D/2013/45/285 - ISBN 978 94 014 1082 3 – NUR 801

Book design: Marco Cassano & Peer De Maeyer
Christof Verelst & Kris Thys
Editorship: Sara Reymen (Woord & Beeld)
SIM Belgium

© Jan Kriekels & Lannoo Publishers nv, Tielt, 2013.

LannooCampus Publishers is a subsidiary of Lannoo Publishers,
the book and multimedia division of Lannoo Publishers nv

LannooCampus Publishers
Erasme Ruelensvest 179, box 101
3001 Leuven
Belgium

www.lannoocampus.be

INNOVATE OR DIE

THE UNIVERSAL SURVIVAL PHILOSOPHY OF
JAN KRIEKELS

JAGA VALUE TOTEM

MESSAGE
- OUT OF THE FUTURE -

ABOUT JAN KRIEKELS

AN ECCENTRIC, A REBEL, A DREAMER. That is how I often get described in interviews. But that is putting it a bit simply perhaps ... although it is not entirely incorrect. The path that I have chosen to take throughout my life has been anything but straight-forward. There have been a lot of twists and turns along the way, and I have taken a few side roads too. And above all, I've gone off the beaten track many a time.

The moment I first set eyes on a map of the world is one I will remember forever. A four-year-old boy suddenly discovered that there was more to the world than the Die-penbeek market square ... that was a revelation. And I soon felt that it was an insult to our planet to ignore all those different, interesting countries out there; I could not un-derstand those who had no desire to discover the world outside their village. The first time I heard the word 'Fiji' was a turning point: I wanted to see the world and not just hear others talking about it. This urge to explore would know no bounds, something that could have been predicted even then. Working, eating and sleeping ... that would never be enough for me. There is much more to life than that.

The two role models in my early childhood – my father and my mother – showed me you can choose from a number of different directions in life. My father was the em-bodiment of the hard worker's ethic. He was an ingenious engineer. Giving up was simply not a part of his vocabulary. And he wanted to pass these qualities onto me. He always set me to work; sitting still was not an option. He would be welding with my uncle in the workshop behind our house, day in, day out. They had a company that installed central heating, and later convectors: Gebroeders Kriekels ('Kriekels Broth-ers'). They later changed the name to Jaga, using the first two letters of their respective names: Jan and Gaston. In those early years, I would sometimes help out and I did it with enthusiasm and an entrepreneurial spirit. At the age of 11, I was already carrying out heating trials in the garage.

My mother's family provided me with quite different insights. Speech and discourse were the greatest goods according to that side of the family. I got my creativity from my mother, as well as the urge to keep looking for the ideal, to fight for the things that seemed impossible to achieve. Her brother was the polar opposite of my father in every respect. He played the guitar and would sit around musing all day, writing books and philosophising about the cosmos, the Muses and the meaning of life. This showed me that you could do things differently ... The economic and technical ideas on the one hand, the artistic and philosophical way of life on the other. These ele-ments continued to recur in my circle of friends later in life. And in the end, it was precisely that juxtaposition which made me who I am.

Although I would go on to travel the world in my adult life, my first trip as a child was one of the most memorable. When I was four years old, I hid in my father's van before dawn. In the morning, the van set off for a construction site in Brussels. He let me help out the whole day, but when we came home late at night, the house was in uproar. My mother was furious; she had raised the alarm all over the neighbourhood. This first form of escapism was the harbinger of my rebellious youth.

During my teens, I got bored quickly. My urge to explore the world was immense. I started backpacking in my holidays. I would travel by plane to a far-flung destination and start exploring on arrival. I planned everything myself and hitch-hiked from one place to the next. I had to work for a long time to be able to buy a plane ticket, but once I had arrived at my destination, life was cheap. I didn't need luxury and comfort. I didn't sleep in hotels, but would rather lose myself in nature. I wanted to discover real life and immerse myself in new cultures.

My travelling was made all the more special by a sense of timelessness. This feeling would envelope me wherever I went. The intriguing contact with other cultures and my lack of a plan meant I completely lost all sense of time. That feeling was unique and I still cherish it. The fact that nobody really knew where I was also made my travel experiences all the more extraordinary. I often had no contact with family or friends for months on end. This further intensified the feeling of freedom.

Since my childhood, I have been driven by a wide-ranging curiosity. When the time came to start studying, I didn't limit myself to one discipline. I took psychology, engineering, anthropology, philosophy, design and economics. But I also wanted to continue discovering how different other cultures are, with my own eyes. I travelled all over the world: from Mongolia and Indonesia to South America, Mexico and the United States. The things I experienced were to determine my vision for the future.

For example, in the region around Wamema in Papua (known as Irian Jaya at the time) on the island of New Guinea, I got to know a population that explicitly identified itself with nature. I observed the people of the small villages in the Maoke Mountains and took part in their daily life and rituals. I didn't need to speak the language to communicate. I showed humility by offering food to the mothers. They divided that among the families and gave me cooked food in return. It was always a risk to make myself so dependent on them, but this created trust, which allowed me a glimpse of their traditions and customs.

One day I took a long road back to the spot where a pilot had dropped me off a few weeks earlier and would pick me up and take me back to Biak. Until then, my courage had known no bounds, but a new feeling came over me on that road: fear. On an island where headhunters who had been expelled from the villages laid down the law, I was walking in the dark through the woods. My senses had never been so sharp. I ended up making that journey four times. It was only on the fourth day that the plane came to collect me.

I built my first house – in the United States – all thanks to a certain coincidence. I was hitch-hiking when a Jaguar suddenly pulled up. The lady behind the wheel agreed to give me a ride but along the way her car broke down. I managed to repair it and she offered me a job on the spot: to build a house. And so I built a huge villa for her – right in the middle of an earthquake region – along with 35 other people, mainly Mexican day labourers. That project taught me a lot.

At one point while travelling in South America, I had been sitting on top of a moving truck full of worn cobblestones for several hours. It was about 45 degrees Celsius and I was in a semi-trance because of the constant swaying of the truck. After four hours I turned around and was just able to duck in time as we drove under a bridge. That's when I realised that man has a kind of super-sensory basic consciousness, which only awakes in the most extreme conditions.

In Mongolia, I spent three gruelling weeks at the other extreme, in temperatures of –20 degrees Celsius. It was only then that I fully realised that heat is a vital necessity and a beautiful gift, because quality of life is simply impossible without it. You only realise that when it is no longer there. Back home after X months away, I joined the family business with a new attitude and a different perspective. I had been searching for a purpose ... and in that extreme cold, I found it.

I started working for Jaga in the beginning of the eighties – and the oil crisis. High energy prices almost spelled the end for the company and led to a turning point. In retrospect, this was the ideal time for me to start because people are more open to innovation in times of crisis. And radical innovation in all areas was just what I wanted; innovation was my driving force. I had to make products that didn't exist yet. Conservatism was – and still is – my biggest enemy; I will never repeat myself.

At Jaga, I got to know all of the departments up close, but it soon became clear that product development was my hobby-horse. My father and I started with the production of ecological heat pumps. Oil was expensive, so we decided to make heat from the ambient air. Jaga devoted ever more attention to energy efficiency and the design of less polluting products. As a result Jaga was successful, despite times of economic difficulty. The small company that had once started as Gebroeders Kriekels was now a market leader in heat pumps. Jaga would go on to permanently replace the polluting central heating boiler.

At the end of the eighties, I began to realise that Jaga was not offering enough special products to really stand out. Our technology was excellent, but we weren't as good at design. This meant that Jaga remained a local company with increasingly narrower margins. With each day, it became harder to keep our heads above water. We needed a different approach. The decision that my father and I made was unique and daring at that time: customised products. Jaga started making heating products for specific target groups such as hospitals. We did away with the serial production of the early years and the proven methods used by our competitors. Jaga let the customers make their own choices, opted for *prosumption* and differentiation, and started selling niche products.

To me, innovation doesn't just mean developing new products. It also means international expansion. I started presenting the Jaga catalogue abroad with the help of interpreters. We went to Germany, Estonia, the former Czechoslovakia and Russia. These had been unexplored areas within our industry. At the same time I started looking for new marketing techniques and opted for *experience branding*. I wanted customers to experience our brand. We needed more emphasis on creativity and emotion, rather than promoting purely commercial factors. I didn't want to sell customers a radiator, but rather a feeling. The underlying theory was that Jaga warms your soul, as well as your house. This move to out-of-the-box thinking heralded a drastic change. Since then, the company has taken its own path, without looking at what competitors are doing. And our success has come naturally. Jaga developed the fastest, most efficient radiators in the world and won countless awards. We installed heating systems in the Federation Towers in Moscow, the residential accommodation of Russian President Vladimir Putin, the headquarters of Telefónica in Madrid and thousands of other buildings. Sales rose steadily, exports went through the roof. In 2003, Jaga was awarded the 'Export Lion' award.[1]

Managing a company turned out to be much easier than surviving in nature. During my world travels, I constantly had to be innovative. It was often a matter of innovate or die. I had to let go of the situation and quickly think of a solution, or I would have had it. I have taken all those memories and experiences with me along the way. They have made me the person I am today. I have been able to translate them into my work for the company, and now they constitute the very heart of the company's philosophy and of Jaga's products. The company's mission and vision include the same elements

---

1   Annual prize awarded by Flanders Investment & Trade to Flemish companies.

as my personal philosophies. There is room for nature, emotions, design, spirituality, cooperation and dreams. Sometimes these different facets collide with each other, but that is always enriching. I have learned to let go too. At the point when I know something through and through, I start to learn about something new. This helps me stay young and alert, and it means that Jaga is constantly reinventing itself.

I am both a teacher and a student. The path I have taken to making my dreams come true has rendered me wiser and more fulfilled. In this book, I describe five values derived from my outlook on life, my travel experiences and my business philosophies. To me, they form the absolute basis of a better, more sustainable future.

An eccentric? A rebel? A dreamer? Maybe. But if I were able to write my introduction in interviews myself from now on, I would choose: a creative economist. Or better still: an innovator.

INNOVATION. *The* word of the twenty-first century. There has never been as much in-novation going on as there is now. And there has never been as much demand for it. A bizarre paradox. So are we innovating in the most effective way?

Life on our planet is changing dramatically. Sooner rather than later, we need to look for new ways to survive. Innovation today should serve just one goal: the quest for a universal survival model. This is the only way that our future can be guaranteed.

FIVE BASIC VALUES

For me, true innovation is contained in ancient principles. I created my survival phi-losophy based on five key values that I gleaned from my experiences, education and business philosophies. We all know these values, but we have to dig deep in our con-sciousness these days to discover their origins. And yet these basic principles contain the renewal that we – and our planet – so crave. By reactivating these basic values, we are laying down a new, more sustainable path to the future. These five values are our new foundation:

VALUE 1	**RESPECT NATURE**	VALUE 4	**CREATE EMOTION**
VALUE 2	**AWAKE THE ARTIST**	VALUE 5	**BUILD BRIDGES**
VALUE 3	**DREAM A FUTURE**		

INTELLIGENCE, EMOTION AND SPIRITUALITY

The five values are based on three components, which are present in everyone: intelli-gence, emotion and spirituality. The first three values – *Respect Nature, Awake the Artist* and *Dream a Future* – are the simplest for Westerners to adopt. We mainly use the left-hand side of our brain for these – the same side as logic, reason, facts, and evidence. The other two are a throwback to the emotional and spiritual person within. To fully understand them and to realise their importance, we must appeal to the right-hand side of our brain. We have to open ourselves up to something that we may not be able to grasp immediately.

At this moment, man is being confronted with the terrible consequences of some-thing he himself has caused. His negative impact on the planet is becoming more evident every day. Now he must prove his worth – and he can't do that just with the mathematical mind that has dominated thinking in modern times. We need more creativity, emotion and a collective dream. And above all, we need a sense of belong-ing that makes committed collaboration possible, so that we can realise our dream for the future.

AWAKE
THE ARTIST

RESPECT
NATURE

DREAM
A FUTURE

CREATE
EMOTION

BUILD
BRIDGES

FIVE ARCHETYPES

I link one archetype to each basic value, making five archetypes in total. These archetypes are present in every society and, to a certain extent, in every human being. My thinking has been inspired by the principles of the ancient tribes, because the combination of various characteristics enabled these tribes to survive. A monoculture died out. Even today, these five archetypes need to be represented in every layer of society. This means that every company needs to have them too, to really innovate. By allowing these different characters to work together openly and critically, we are laying the foundations for sustainable results and future-oriented decisions.

VALUE 1
Respect Nature – the Green Engineer
He respects nature and the circle of life.

VALUE 2
Awake the Artist – the Artist
He awakes the artist within us.

VALUE 3
Dream a Future – the Visionary
He dreams about our future and builds
the sustainable path to achieving it.

VALUE 4
Create Emotion – the Motivator
He creates emotion and inspires us to
cooperate.

VALUE 5
Build Bridges – the Navigator
He builds bridges between our spirits.

A SUSTAINABLE ALTERNATIVE

In this book, I present an alternative to every outmoded way of thinking and every tried and tested method. Right now, we have one foot in the old world and the other in the new. The transition is already in full flow. That's why there is both a hard and a soft copy of my book; it acts as a bridge between what we know and where we want to go.

I want to use this book to contribute to a better way of living and a more sustainable way of doing business. I want to use my alternative path for each value to show that innovation is feasible. I want to show that things can be done differently – no, *have* to be done differently. We are the last generation that can still make a difference. Innovation is no longer a choice but an absolute necessity. It is up to us: innovate or die ...

RESPECT NATURE

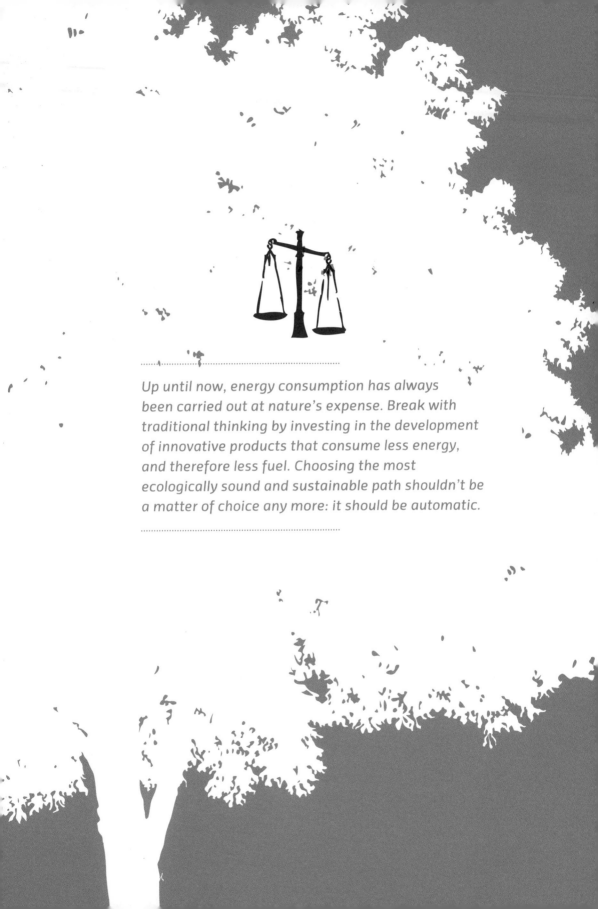

Up until now, energy consumption has always been carried out at nature's expense. Break with traditional thinking by investing in the development of innovative products that consume less energy, and therefore less fuel. Choosing the most ecologically sound and sustainable path shouldn't be a matter of choice any more: it should be automatic.

FIRE = EVOLUTION?

The source of human civilisation as we know it is fire. Fire determined the strength of the human being. Fire is the engine of everything; fire and burning have catapulted man from zero to hero. A life without fuel is unthinkable these days ...

Nevertheless, of the four basic elements, fire has also proven to be the most devastating. Our water, our air and our earth feel its impact every day.

The question of whether fire has enabled human evolution is therefore central in this first section, because my first value – *Respect Nature* – demands respect for all four natural elements: earth, water, air and fire, and it is technology that connects them all.

Going way back in time is part of my quest for answers: to the foundations of Western civilisation. According to Greek mythology, man was given fire by Prometheus, who stole it from the gods of Olympus. It soon emerged that his gift was not all that it seemed ...

THE MYTH OF FIRE: PROMETHEUS' STOLEN GIFT

Fire was invaluable to the Greek gods. When Prometheus stole a lighted torch from Olympus, the consequences were far-reaching. Prometheus gave fire from the gods to mankind because he saw that man was unhappy. This act meant he incurred the wrath of the almighty Zeus, who punished him by chaining him up on a mountain. An eagle came every day to feast on his liver, but as Zeus made it grow back each night, the eagle would simply return the following day.

The Olympic flame The Olympic flame originated from this myth: the Romans kept the flame in the temple of Zeus burning throughout the games to keep the memory of the theft alive. The tradition of carrying the flame is still an integral part of every Olympic Games.

Fire in human hands Thanks to his act of thievery, Prometheus played a key role in the history of mankind, because humans went on to make good use of that stolen gift. Fire was the basis of a true transformation: man evolved from a low, insignificant creature to an almost divine creation. The ability to deal with fire in a responsible way meant a drastic change in human ways of living. People were able to warm themselves. They were better equipped to keep wildlife at a distance, as animals appeared to have a primal fear of fire. They could also use flames to sharpen spears, which made hunting easier. They roasted meat and were able to eat a more varied diet, which allowed them to ingest nutrients more quickly. Human health and life expectancy thus

FIRE IS EVOLUTION

?

also improved significantly. Improved living conditions and more free time meant the human brain could develop.

Pandora's Box: all the sins of the world Zeus didn't just punish Prometheus for his betrayal; he also punished man. He sent Pandora to bring disaster on them. Pandora was given many good gifts by the gods: Athena gave her intelligence and talent and Aphrodite gave her the beauty of a goddess. Hermes, however, gave her the gift of speech, a deceitful nature and shameless thoughts. She also had a characteristic that was to have terrible consequences: curiosity. Zeus gave Pandora to Prometheus' brother along with a box that contained all the misfortune of the world. The curious Pandora opened the box and brought disease and disaster to the earth. She tried to close the lid quickly, but the only thing still left inside the box was hope.

Fire as a symbol Prometheus means *the forward-thinking one*. Fire could therefore be a symbol for inspiration and intelligence because, thanks to altered living conditions, humans suddenly had the ability to think about more than simply surviving. There was now room for deeper thoughts and ideas. Thanks to the advances brought about by fire, humans developed far more swiftly than other living beings on earth. In *The Secret Doctrine*, HP Blavatsky refers to the myth of Prometheus as 'the allegory of the pilgrimage of man, in which thought is the hero who overcomes evil forces and eventually regains a state of wisdom and freedom'.

Evolution? The crucial question is whether man has really used that wisdom to improve his lot. And whether he has seized his new freedom as an opportunity to create a better future ... I don't think the answer is a definite 'no' just yet – although I do think that moment is getting closer. It is clear that humans have not dealt with Prometheus' gift in the most efficient way. Yet we now need to carry on with the hope that remained in Pandora's Box, because that will be imperative to ensuring our ability to survive.

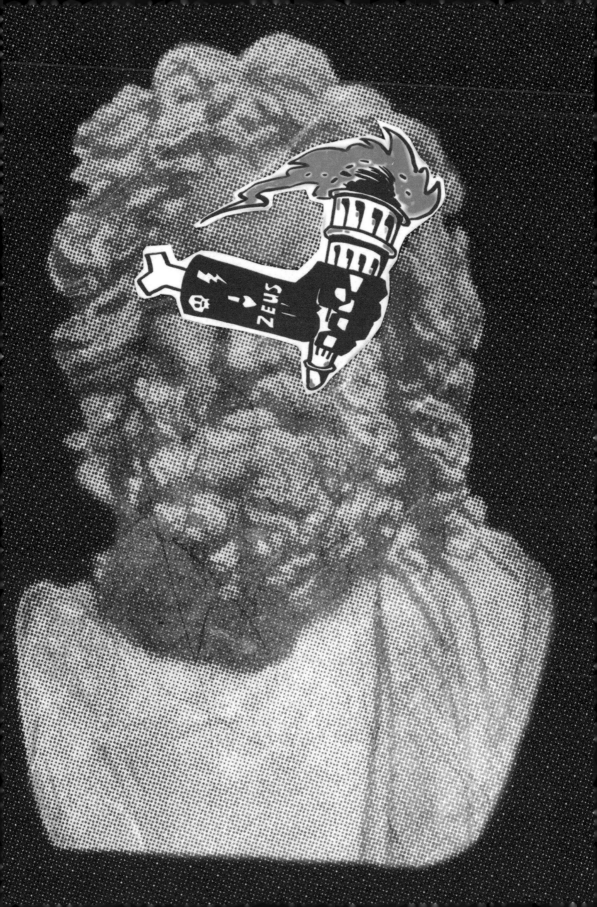

FROM MYTH TO REALITY: THE EARTH IS SUFFERING

I believe respecting nature starts with one crucial insight, which is that the earth did create a perfect equilibrium once upon a time. This was a balanced system that made millions of life forms possible. For a long time, man was just one of many small components. Then, one day, he disturbed that unique equilibrium and irreversibly affected all ecosystems designed so carefully by the earth. Man's decisions formed the basis of a profound change for nature: global warming and a drastic change in the habitat of all life forms. In short, this wasn't just climate change but a profound modification of our biotope.

Climate change and a system thrown off balance

AN AGE-OLD PHENOMENON   Climate change has been an issue at various stages throughout the history of the earth. Average temperatures rise and fall, air currents and water cycles change... the climate and weather are constantly changing. During the ice ages, it was significantly colder on earth than it is today, but there have also been periods when the average temperature was a lot higher. Some changes in climate came about gradually, whereas others came about more quickly and had a major impact on the earth, although this was not as high everywhere.

Changing weather conditions has different causes. For example, a change in solar activity can temporarily affect temperatures. The 'Little Ice Age' in Europe – between 1600 and 1800 – was caused by this. Even volcanic eruptions affect the weather. The ash and sulphur released during an eruption block the sun's rays and cause a slightly lower temperature for a number of years. Changes in ocean currents and air currents also influence the weather. For example, the El Niño phenomenon, in which sea water along the equator in the eastern Pacific Ocean warms up, is directly related to local rainfall.

THE BALANCE: THE GREENHOUSE EFFECT AND PHOTOSYNTHESIS The temperature on earth – and therefore the weather – is closely related to two natural processes: global warming and photosynthesis. Our planet uses both to maintain a balance in nature.

GREENHOUSE EFFECT: THE EARTH UNDER A BELL JAR The interplay between the sun, atmosphere and earth determines the temperature on the planet. The sun gives off rays to the earth, which in turn sends the heat from the sun's rays back into the atmosphere. Some of these leave the atmosphere immediately; the others are absorbed by the earth, which re-radiates the energy in the form of infrared radiation or heat. It is this radiation that is partially absorbed by gases which occur naturally in the atmosphere. This creates the effect of a conservatory or greenhouse: the heat is retained, so the temperature rises. Carbon dioxide (CO_2) and methane (CH_4) – the most important of the so-called greenhouse gases – play an important role in this effect. Thanks to the greenhouse effect, the average temperature on earth is about 15 degrees Celsius, rather than –18. In other words, this process makes life possible.

PHOTOSYNTHESIS: CO_2 TURNS INTO OXYGEN Nature maintains its own balance by controlling the amount of carbon dioxide in the atmosphere by way of photosynthesis. Plants use light energy to absorb CO_2 and to turn it into oxygen. They also form carbohydrates from the CO_2 and water. This means that the flora on earth is crucial to life. Forests and seas are carbon dioxide warehouses and they act as the lungs of our earth. They reduce the amount of CO_2 in the air, which means the atmosphere does not warm up too much. In short, they keep the planet cool and ensure that the system remains stable.

The greenhouse effect and photosynthesis are, in other words, two natural processes which together keep temperatures on earth under control and optimise the composition of our air – or rather, that's what happens if they are able to carry out their work as normal. Throughout the centuries, other natural processes have had an impact on this balanced cooperation, but nature has always managed to repair itself. Until now.

THE DIFFERENCE TODAY: ANTHROPOGENIC CHANGE
The current climate change is unlike any previous one. Scientists have thought long and hard about this for decades, as twentieth century climate change could not be fully explained by natural processes. The conclusion was rather obvious: human activity was the basis of the change. This conclusion launched a period of contention and discussion between scientists, industrialists and policymakers, given the enormity of its economic, ecological and political consequences.

Man has unbalanced the system. Humans have caused climate change.

The first step towards recognising the problem has been taken. No one would really dare to openly doubt its existence: climate change is a fact and man has caused it. However, although the period for discussions and expressing doubt may well be a thing of the past, effective measures to tackle the problem have still not been forthcoming from our world leaders and policymakers, despite the fact that the time for action is now! I can only hope that humanity and nature don't have to wait too much longer for us to finally sit up and take note, and that we don't have to wake up one day and realise that it's too late to resolve the situation.

The turning point: the Industrial Revolution It didn't take scientists long to establish the point at which the system of global warming and photosynthesis was disturbed: the end of the eighteenth century. The Industrial Revolution thus became not only a turning point in the history of man, but also in that of nature.

GAS	EMISSION FROM
Carbon dioxide (CO$_2$)	• Combustion of fossil fuels for electricity and heat • Forest fires • Burning agricultural waste • Transport • Thawing of permafrost
Methane (CH$_4$)	• Livestock farming • Rice cultivation • Gas leakages in the coal, oil and gas industry • Thawing of permafrost
Black carbon (soot or particulate matter)	• Burning forests and grasslands • Burning agricultural waste and firewood • Transport with diesel engines without emission filters
Halogenated alkanes	• Industry
Carbon monoxide (CO) and volatile organic hydrocarbons	• Combustion of biomass • Industry • Cars and trucks (especially in the US)
Nitrogen oxide (N$_2$O)	• Fertilisers in agriculture

300

CO₂
PARTS PER MILLION

250

Temperature
DEGREES CELSIUS
VE/BELOW CURRENT

0
-2°C
-4°C
-8°C

SEA LEVEL
-20 m (-65.8 ft)
-40 m
-60 m
-80 m

Sea level
METERS ABOVE OR
BELOW CURRENT

400,000 YEARS AGO   300,000

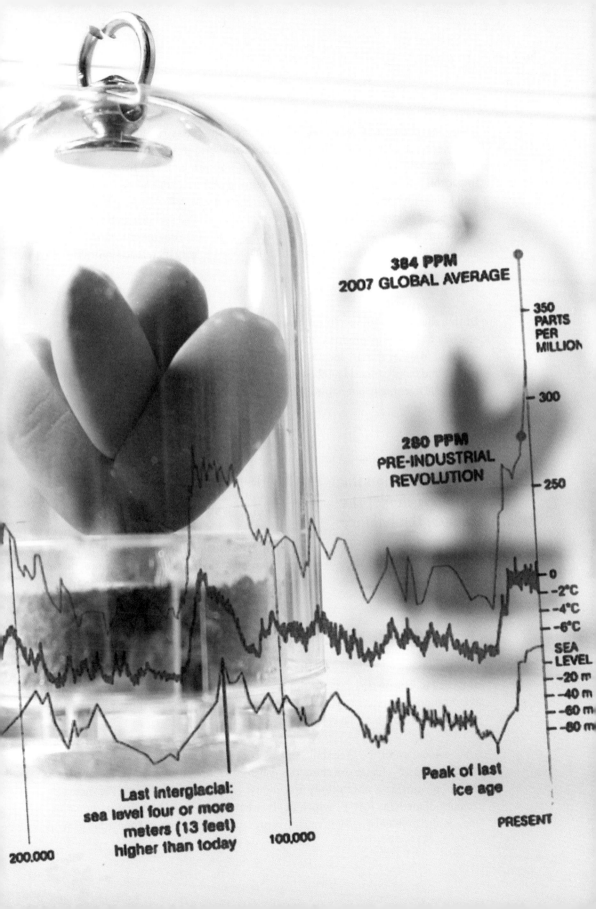

384 PPM
2007 GLOBAL AVERAGE

350
PARTS
PER
MILLION

300

280 PPM
PRE-INDUSTRIAL
REVOLUTION

250

0
-2°C
-4°C
-6°C

SEA
LEVEL

-20 m
-40 m
-60 m
-80 m

Peak of last
ice age

Last interglacial:
sea level four or more
meters (13 feet)
higher than today

PRESENT

200,000   100,000

A DIFFERENT LIFE FOR MAN AND FOR NATURE The Industrial Revolution affected nearly every aspect of daily life in the Western World in particular. The transition from manual labour to production by machines running on fuel had an enormous impact on how things were done. The invention of the steam engine meant objects could suddenly be produced quickly and in large quantities; coal mining gave an additional boost to steel production; factories and cities started sprouting up everywhere and forests had to make room for more factories; and steam engines running on wood and coal worked at full speed, meaning production capacity increased significantly.

OPTING FOR MORE TIME OR MORE PRODUCTION

During the Industrial Revolution man made an important decision. The speed and efficiency of machine production gave him the opportunity to invest the time he had regained in other things, such as personal development and keeping in touch with friends and family. Instead he chose to produce more, and it was this mass production that would eventually put natural processes under pressure.

Man has changed the composition of the atmosphere: the balance has been disturbed.

A BALANCED SYSTEM BECOMES OUT OF KILTER Since the Industrial Revolution, humans have been emitting increasing amounts of greenhouse gases into the air – in particular carbon dioxide (CO_2), which is primarily emitted by burning fossil fuels for energy, heat and transport. Massive deforestation in recent centuries means we have fewer green areas to fulfil the purifying function of photosynthesis. This is how more and more carbon dioxide is emitted into the air. Humans have changed the composition of the atmosphere dramatically over the past two centuries.

MORE AND MORE GREENHOUSE GASES It is this increase of the amount of greenhouse gases in the atmosphere that causes global warming. The gases work like a kind of braking system, which prevents the earth from getting rid of the sun's heat as easily as it used to. This means that our thin atmosphere becomes increasingly thicker and retains more infrared rays. This in turn warms up the lower atmospheric layers while the highest atmospheric layers get less heat.

The best known of the greenhouse gases is carbon dioxide. Discussions about addressing climate change are therefore usually about how to reduce CO_2 emissions. Yet carbon dioxide is not the only greenhouse gas that causes damage. The increased amount of methane (CH_4) – which holds twenty times more heat than carbon dioxide – is also problematic. Methane is mainly emitted by livestock. Population growth

means meat production has increased and the amount of methane in the air continues to rise. Other greenhouse gases with a heavy impact on nature's balance include black carbon, halogenated alkanes, nitrogen oxide, carbon monoxide and volatile organic hydrocarbons.

The production of electricity and heat is responsible for a quarter of greenhouse gas emissions. Deforestation ranks second at 18 per cent. Transport, industry and agriculture also contribute to pollution – each is responsible for about 14 per cent of emissions.

REDUCED LUNG CAPACITY OF THE EARTH The earth's surface consists of about four billion hectares of forest: that is about one third of the total land area. Deforestation has been going on for centuries, but it has been taking place ever more frequently in recent decades. This creates a twofold problem: more carbon dioxide and fewer purifying trees.

The destruction of forests is responsible for around one fifth of annual carbon dioxide emissions. Forests are burned for agricultural purposes, like establishing plantations and livestock farming. Brazil and Indonesia in particular are engaging in deforestation on a large scale. In Indonesia, this is done in order to establish palm oil plantations. More forest is felled and the land is drained by setting fire to the peat. The palm oil is used for the food industry and for the production of biodiesel, although this last usage is coming increasingly under fire. This is because a life cycle analysis spanning several years showed that the entire process for the production of this biofuel emits more carbon dioxide into the air than the plantations can extract from it.

Deforestation thus contributes to global warming in two ways. On the one hand, trees that are destroyed emit carbon dioxide and this goes into the atmosphere. On the other hand, there are fewer trees to extract carbon dioxide from the air and turn it into oxygen. In short, just when the earth needs a good set of lungs more than ever, it has to deal with a reduced lung capacity.

CONSTANTLY ON THE LOOKOUT FOR MORE ENERGY Where do we get the fossil fuels that pollute our earth? Well, paradoxically, from the earth itself. The earth's crust was formed during the Precambrian era, which began 4.56 billion years ago. There was a lot of volcanic activity and a lot of meteorites and comets hit the earth. At the beginning of this period, the atmosphere consisted mainly of carbon dioxide, methane and ammonia. At a later stage, the atmosphere cooled down rapidly since almost all of the methane had disappeared from it. In recent centuries, humans started to mine the oil and gas supplies, hidden in the depths of the earth, which originated during this period. They opened up Pandora's Box ...

The amount of fossil fuels that we need today to meet our basic needs is increasing all the time. We now need more energy to achieve the same effect, simply because our energy fields are further and further away. The result is entropy, a drastic depreciation. We used up the resources in our immediate vicinity – such as the wood of the forests we lived in – quite quickly. This meant we had to get energy out of the ground: lignite, coal, oil, gas. We had to look ever deeper to find these fossil fuels. We made it more and more difficult for ourselves and so we also needed more complex technology. The scarcer the resources became, the more risks we took, all for the sake of comfort and lifestyle and to be able to keep up with population growth. The result is an increasingly large ecological footprint and an ever-growing water footprint *(see box, page 48 & 54).*

Our climate: from stable to variable Greenhouse gas levels and global temperatures have fluctuated since the planet came into existence. Scientists established this by examining the isotope ratio of oxygen in sludge from the ocean floor. Their research produced data on evaporation and precipitation, and therefore on temperature. The fluctuation of the carbon dioxide concentration in the atmosphere was investigated by analysing air bubbles in ancient ice formations. The Belgian Princess Elisabeth polar station in Antarctica plays an important role in this type of research on glaciers and the climate.

The conclusions of these scientific studies are striking. Over the past 3,000 years, the level of greenhouse gases in the atmosphere has remained fairly stable, as has the average temperature. This biological balance has allowed human civilisation to make such a huge leap forwards. It is only since we began burning fossil fuels *en masse* and emitting greenhouse gases into the atmosphere in many other ways, that we started seeing significant changes.

INSEPARABLE: CO_2, TEMPERATURE AND SEA LEVELS The relationship between carbon dioxide levels, temperature and sea levels is unmistakable: they rise and fall together. It is common knowledge that CO_2 emissions started increasing dramatically from the Industrial Revolution onwards, yet current statistics are staggering. We emit around thirty billion tonnes of carbon dioxide into the atmosphere every year. Nature absorbs half of this and the other half is what causes the increased concentration of CO_2 in the atmosphere.

Our climate has remained fairly constant since the last ice age, which took place some 11,000 years ago. Carbon dioxide levels have never risen above 300 ppm during the past 650,000 years. [Ppm stands for 'parts per million', the number of particles of carbon dioxide in each million of other particles.] Almost two and a half centuries ago, things started to change: we went from 280 ppm in the middle of the eighteenth century to 385 ppm, where we are now. This means that the amount of carbon dioxide in the atmosphere has risen by more than a third since the Industrial Revolution. As well as this, annual global greenhouse gas emissions have increased by up to six billion tonnes since the start of the nineties – a growth of more than 20 per cent!

The average temperature has already risen by about 0.8 degrees Celsius. A study by the UN Environment Programme shows that the period from 2000 to 2009 saw the highest ever greenhouse gas emissions, and this decade was also the warmest ever. The results of the Intergovernmental Panel on Climate Change (IPCC) show an average temperature rise of 0.15 to 0.20 degrees Celsius in each decade. The sea level also increased as rising temperatures melted the ice on glaciers and ice caps. The impact that humans have had on the planet in recent decades is bigger than ever. During the years to come this will not only affect nature and our biotope, but every living creature on this planet.

A temperature increase with serious consequences It is already clear that global warming affects all parts of the world. We come across headlines about devastating hurricanes, severe floods, disastrous droughts and fires when reading our newspapers at breakfast. Climate change has serious consequences for the health of our ecosystems and the conservation of our flora and fauna. The impact grows with each degree that the temperature rises *(see box, page 57).*

Humans and nature will feel the impact of global warming all over the world.

RISING SEA LEVELS The rise in sea levels due to the melting of glaciers and ice caps will have consequences for the world of the future: coasts will become uninhabitable, large parts of the civilised world will be flooded. The effects of climate change are already a painful reality for the people of Kiribati, a volcanic island group in the Pacific Ocean. The islands are just a few centimetres above sea level, which makes increased rainfall, more frequent storms and rising sea levels a constant threat to their survival. Groundwater is salinated, causing difficulties in growing crops. The islanders have already had to move some of their villages.

MORE EXTREME WEATHER The weather is set to become even more extreme and unpredictable. This is because the temperature of the oceans is increasing. In the foreseeable future, strongly rising convection currents and higher wind speeds will start to form above warm water, causing severe storms, hurricanes and tornadoes. Increased evaporation also means more rainfall. In the last two decades of the twentieth century, we saw an increase of 230 per cent of the number of disasters caused by floods. Droughts follow periods of intense rainfall. This creates more forest fires,

THERE IS NO PLANET B

which brings everything that is harmful to the earth's surface. The result is more carbon dioxide in the atmosphere.

SCARCITY OF DRINKING WATER   Climate change has also had an impact on our drinking water supply. Humans only drink fresh water, which comes mainly from melting glaciers. Just 2.75 per cent of all water on earth is fresh and just over 2 per cent of that comes from glaciers. An ice cap acts like a mirror for the sun: it reflects 90 per cent of the rays; thus these are not converted into heat. The sea does, however, absorb a lot of heat. The consequences are obvious: the less ice there is, the faster the temperature rises and the faster the ice disappears. The glaciers are melting away at an alarming rate.

Our water supplies are dwindling. The depletion of water resources has tripled in the past fifty years. Nowadays, 80 per cent of the population lives in an area with a high risk of water shortage. It is becoming increasingly difficult to supply people all over the world with drinking water. By 2050, more than 600 million people will no longer have access to clean water. Water shortages are expected to be particularly acute in the Middle East and Australia.

ECOSYSTEMS ARE AT RISK, BIODIVERSITY IS DECREASING   Climate zones are shifting and entire ecosystems are thus being undermined: the habitat of certain plants and animals is either disappearing or changing radically. Rivers are drying up, forests are withering away. Some life forms are threatened with extinction because they cannot adapt quickly enough. Increasing pollution exacerbates this precarious situation. The Living Planet Report 2012 by the WWF contains shocking figures. The Living Planet Index – which shows the health of our ecosystems and is based on 8,000 groups of 2,500 vertebrate species – shows that biodiversity in the tropics has decreased by 60 per cent since the seventies, and that the natural habitat of many species has also shrunk since the eighties. One fifth of vertebrate species is at risk of extinction. The rhinoceros, orang-utan, gorilla and tiger are among those on the list of endangered (or critically endangered) species.

The situation is no less disturbing in the oceans. Oceans absorb carbon dioxide, which affects biological systems as CO_2 uptake increases the acidity of the oceans. Some marine animals, such as shellfish and corals, suffer the painful consequences of this. The condition of coral reefs has declined by 38 per cent during the past thirty years. Extensive pollution means the cod and river dolphin are now also endangered species.

SEA LEVELS ARE RISING

MORE EXTREME WEATHER

OUR ECOLOGICAL FOOTPRINT

The term *ecological footprint* refers to the impact of our activities on the environment or, more specifically, the impact of the greenhouse gases we produce in our daily life by burning fossil fuels in order to produce electricity, heating and transport.

PRIMARY AND SECONDARY FOOTPRINT We distinguish between two different types of footprint: *primary footprint* refers to the CO_2 that we emit when we burn fossil fuels for household use, personal consumption and transport and *secondary footprint* refers to indirect CO_2 emissions. This is related to the life cycle of the products we use.

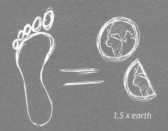

1,5 x earth

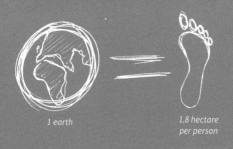

1 earth

1,8 hectare per person

BIOSPHERE AND BIOCAPACITY Scientists can use the ecological footprint to compare the influence of humans on the biosphere to the capacity of the earth to regenerate or restore itself. That ability is called the *biocapacity* of the earth. It is linked to the amount of natural resources that the planet gives us in the form of forests, rivers, farmland and fish stocks … Global hectares are used as a unit of measure. The total biocapacity of the earth is 11.9 billion. This means each person should have no more than approximately 1.8 hectares.

AN INCREASINGLY LARGE FOOTPRINT And now for the alarming figures … In 2007, the average ecological footprint was 2.7 hectares per person. This means that we use our natural resources faster than they can recover. In the seventies, mankind was already at the point where the annual ecological footprint was roughly equal to the biocapacity of the planet. After passing that point, the world's population started to consume more than our ecosystems could handle meaning there were more CO_2 emissions than the ecosystem could absorb. This trend is set to continue: figures from 2007 showed that the earth would need a year and a half to absorb CO_2 emissions from that year. In short, humans used the equivalent of 1.5 planets.

NOT ALL FOOTPRINTS ARE EQUAL It is a well-known fact that rich, more developed countries have a larger footprint than poorer, less developed countries. The footprint of an average European is 4.7 hectares, and that of an African just 1.4 hectares. In 2007, the richest 31 countries (OECD countries) were responsible for 37 per cent of the ecological footprint of the entire planet. That is extremely high compared to the ten ASEAN countries and 53 African countries, which were responsible for 12 per cent between them.

THE EVOLUTION OF THE ECOLOGICAL FOOTPRINT

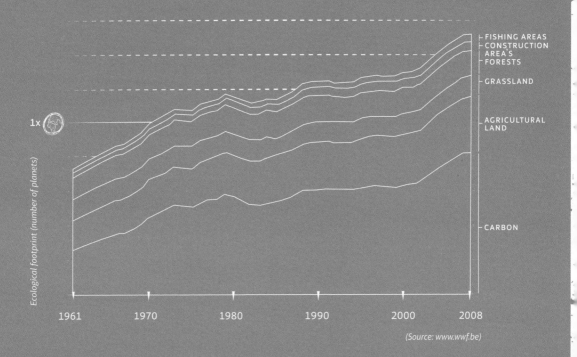

2x

1x

Ecological footprint (number of planets)

FISHING AREAS
CONSTRUCTION AREA'S
FORESTS

GRASSLAND

AGRICULTURAL LAND

CARBON

1961   1970   1980   1990   2000   2008

(Source: www.wwf.be)

TOP 10 - LARGEST ECOLOGICAL FOOTPRINT

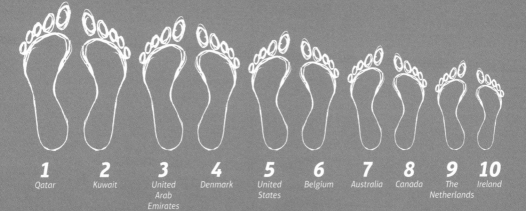

1 Qatar   **2** Kuwait   **3** United Arab Emirates   **4** Denmark   **5** United States   **6** Belgium   **7** Australia   **8** Canada   **9** The Netherlands   **10** Ireland

YOUR PERSONAL ECOLOGICAL FOOTPRINT

You can calculate your own ecological footprint at www.wwf-footprint.be.
Some examples:

A family of four lives in a well-insulated, medium-sized detached house. The family is neither exceptionally lavish nor particularly sparing with its fuel heating and electricity usage. The family members rarely use public transport. They travel between 50 and 100 kilometres by car every day. Once a year, they fly to a European destination for their holidays. The family eats mostly fresh produce, but also canned and frozen vegetables. They eat fish or meat around five times a week. The family mainly uses recycled paper and does not have many leaflets delivered. They do have a subscription to a newspaper.

The ecological footprint of a member of this household is 8.1 hectares.

8.1 hectare = 16 football fields.

Their neighbours, a family of four, love eating out and often have ready-made meals when at home. Their large house is poorly insulated and heated with fuel oil. They pay little attention to their consumption of electricity. The family get a lot of leaflets delivered and several family members have multiple subscriptions to newspapers and magazines. They do their photocopying on white paper. They always travel by car and travel more than 100 kilometres per day. The family likes to travel by plane to exotic destinations.

The ecological footprint of a member of this household is 13.9 hectares.

13.9 hectare = 28 football fields.

The neighbours across the road like to set a good example. They use green energy for their extremely well insulated small house. They are vegetarians and opt for seasonal fruits and vegetables. The family doesn't have a car and they prefer spending their holidays at home. Moreover, the family only uses recycled paper, does not get any leaflets delivered and does not subscribe to any newspapers or magazines.

The ecological footprint of a member of this household is 1.8 hectares

1,8 hectare = 4 football fields.

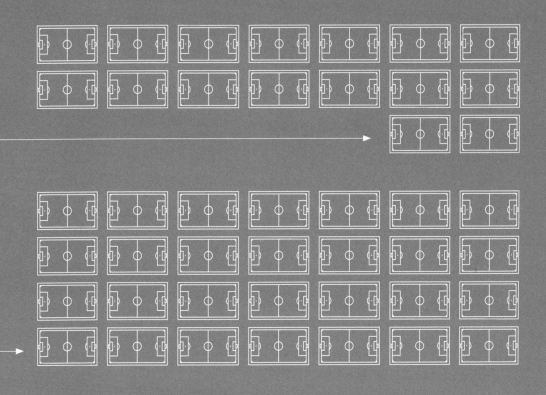

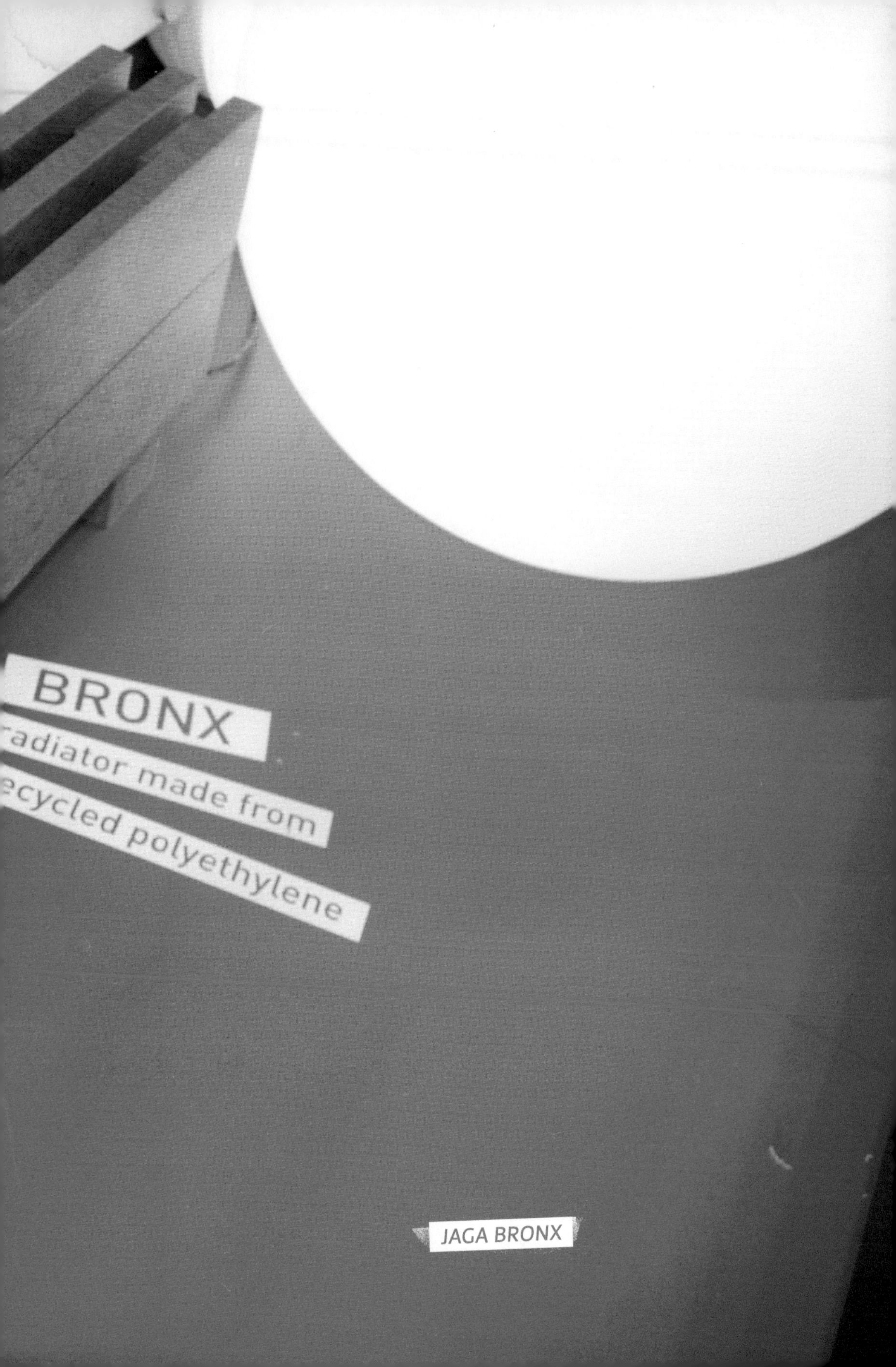

BRONX

radiator made from

ecycled polyethylene

JAGA BRONX

OUR WATER FOOTPRINT

....

Water footprint refers to the amount of water needed to produce an object or food product: from the raw material(s) to the end product you find in shops. The largest water usage is hidden in our food and clothing.

....

WATER FOOTPRINT INCREASINGLY LARGE
What then is the cause of this ever-growing water footprint? This is not only the growing consumerism of humans. The irrigation systems we build to be able to farm on dry land also play an important role. The cultivation of crops often requires more water than is naturally present in the region. The result is that more areas on earth are faced with water-related concerns. The ecological balance of water has been disturbed. Rivers do not reach the sea in dry seasons any more, lakes dry out completely. It isn't just developing countries that face water scarcity: there is a global water shortage.

WATER FOODPRINT AND FOOD

Water footprint in l (in Belgium)

For 1 apple (100 g)
For 1 bottle of beer (500 ml)
For 1 pot of coffee (750 ml)
For 1 liter of milk (1000 l)
For 1 fillet (300 g)
For 1 pork steak (300 g)
For 1 block of cheese (500 g)
For 1 beef steak (300 g)

(Source: www.watervoetafdruk.be)

70 liters	**150** liters	**840** liters	**1000** liters	**1170** liters	**1440** liters	**2500** liters	**4500** liters

CENTER-PIVOT IRRIGATION - MA'AN-JORDAN

NOT ALL WATER FOOTPRINTS ARE EQUAL
During the period 1996–2005, the average water footprint was 1,385 m³ per person per year. As with ecological footprints, the difference between rich and poor countries is significant. In some North American states, the water footprint is over 3,000 m³ per person per year, while most African countries remain below 1,000 m³. In China, the average water footprint is 1,071 m³ per person.

A FEVERISH PLANET: THE EFFECTS OF TEMPERATURE INCREASES ON THE EARTH

....

Waiting for consequences? That's a thing of the past. We are already witnessing global warming.

....

A few degrees warmer? No problem! We may associate this with sunbathing and refreshing cocktails. But we're wrong, of course. The earth suffers if its temperature rises by a few extra degrees, just as a person becomes sick if his temperature rises. A person can function fairly well with a fever of one degree. At two degrees, he feels unwell and needs to rest. At three degrees, his health is in a critical condition. An increase of four degrees and he's had it. According to scientists, the limit our planet can take is an increase of six degrees. At the rate we are going, it is likely that greenhouse gas emissions will double during the next fifty years. This would result in a temperature rise of three degrees.

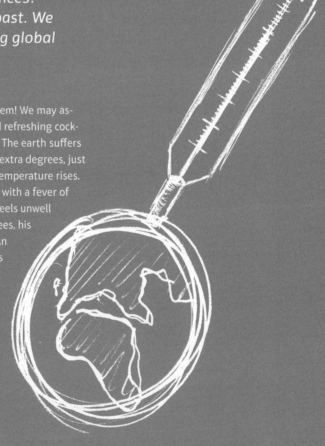

+1°C

THE EFFECTS OF A ONE DEGREE INCREASE Nature and humans adapt quite easily to this. The seasons change: spring begins earlier and winters are milder. The average amount of rainfall increases. The sea level rises. Certain areas benefit from the rise in temperature through increased agricultural yields. Other areas are adversely affected by prolonged periods of drought. We have almost surpassed this level.

+2°C

THE EFFECTS OF A TWO DEGREE INCREASE Certain ecosystems are affected: some animals and plants die out, because they have a limited ability to adapt. Periods of heavy rainfall and massive droughts alternate. Rising sea levels threaten some islands and lowlands. Diseases that previously only occurred in warm areas start to spread. We will witness the effects of this temperature rise in the following decade.

+3°C

THE EFFECTS OF A THREE DEGREE INCREASE Important ecosystems start disappearing and farming becomes difficult in dry areas. Sea levels rise dramatically because the ice sheets on Greenland and Antarctica are melting. The first climate refugees leave their home countries.

+4°C

THE EFFECTS OF A FOUR DEGREE INCREASE The Gulf Stream may come to a standstill. Western Europe starts to cool down. African agricultural yields drop drastically. Some large human migrations start to take place due to droughts and floods in certain areas, resulting in a multitude of social problems.

+5°C

THE EFFECTS OF A FIVE DEGREE INCREASE The last remaining ice disappears from the poles. The Himalayan glaciers no longer exist. Sea levels rise all over the world and seas engulf coastal cities. People start flocking inland where they have less and less space to live. Extreme drought, extreme temperatures and intense rainfall threaten the lives of humans and animals. This results in total chaos.

+6°C

THE EFFECTS OF A SIX DEGREE INCREASE Human life is impossible outside of completely closed off agricultural living bubbles.

A GREENHOUSE LANDSCAPE
OUR WATER FOOTPRINT IS GETTING BIGGER BY THE DAY

CONCLUSION: OUR USE OF FOSSIL FUELS IS NOT EFFICIENT

We are bleeding the earth dry Things started going wrong at the beginning of the Industrial Revolution. Polluting energy became the foundation of our civilisation when the carbon era began. Nature was knocked out of balance. Without the reckless use of oil, gas and coal we would undoubtedly have been in a better position in the twenty-first century. Nowadays, humans are behaving like pyromaniac apes who are slowly burning up the earth. Nature cannot recover because we don't give it the time to do so. The bank account that we are living off is coming ever closer to zero. Scientists use the tragic history of Easter Island as the ultimate example of what will happen to the earth if we just keep sitting and watching: total destruction (*see box, page 63*).

We live in an upside-down world: we consume far more energy than we need.

Entropy: we create decay Man has created scarcity. He cut wood: firstly, to free up land for agriculture, then to build cities. Then he mined coal and lignite. More and more technology was developed in an attempt to control fire. We started looking further afield for our energy sources, and we did that less and less efficiently.

MORE USAGE FOR LESS ENERGY This means that products now cost much more energy to produce than they give. Think of a yoghurt: it contains about 80 kilocalories and provides about an hour's worth of energy, yet it requires at least 10 times as much energy to produce this yoghurt and its packaging and to transport it. This leads to a very dispiriting statistic: 10 calories of energy from fossil fuels are used to produce one calorie of food.

CONTINUOUS LOSS OF VALUE The conclusion is as simple as it is confrontational: we are causing entropy in all areas. More and more energy is being lost and we constantly cause a loss of value, and therefore decay. We are responsible for the inflation of our planet. We are heading into an upside-down world: we are consuming far more energy than we need.

Man is overtaking time

LESS EFFICIENCY, MORE TIME In terms of energy use, human labour and manual production are actually a hundred times more efficient than the use of fossil fuels. This can be shown by making a simple comparison: If a farmer prepares the ground with his horse and plough, then he will put about as much energy into this process as he gets in return. He sows seeds and harvests the produce. The manure from his horse serves as food for the soil. If the same farmer were to start working with his tractor, then he would consume much more energy. He needs fuel, which has to to be mined and transported. The production of his tractor also used up a lot of energy. The only benefits for the farmer are financial gain and saving time.

HUMANS ARE SPEEDING UP, THE PLANET SHOULD FOLLOW And ultimately that is what it is all about: man has tried to overtake time and to live in the future. He has succeeded in this attempt with the help of fire – the gift from the gods. And because he is a creature of habit, he doesn't want to give up comfort. Energy and industrialisation have increased human power. Now that new economies *(see box, page 64)* are ready to participate in that race against time, waiting for alternatives is no longer an option. How much longer can our planet cope with these increasing speed levels?

EASTER ISLAND:
ALL USED UP AND PERISHED

Easter Island or Rapa Nui is a Polynesian island of approximately 160 square kilometres in the Pacific. It is one of the most isolated islands in the world. The history of Easter Island is that of a downward spiral in which a rich and developed culture rapidly perished.

A UNIQUE ECOSYSTEM Easter Island was highly biodiverse: it had unique birds and plants. But due to massive deforestation, rainfall on the island began to increase and this had severe consequences. The population decreased significantly due to famine, warfare and cannibalism. When the population started breeding sheep at the end of the

nineteenth century, this too had an impact on the island's flora. The island, which had once been full of forests, became covered with grass. Complete deforestation, overpopulation and exhaustion of the few natural resources it had, meant the island became impoverished.

THE COLLAPSE OF EASTER ISLAND: A DOOMS-DAY SCENARIO Some historians and biologists see the events of Easter Island as a doomsday picture of what our planet should expect to happen: the demise of a culture due to the complete exhaustion of natural resources. Do we really want to let things go that far?

NEW GLOBAL ECONOMIES

It is well known that the rapid economic growth of countries like China, India, Brazil and Russia is not beneficial for the climate. More demand for energy means more greenhouse gas emissions. And these countries mainly use coal plants with very high CO_2 emissions. For example, 80 per cent of the power plants in China run on coal. The country has also bought up energy companies over the past decades and has stakes in oilfields. The spectacular rate of population growth in these countries is an additional threat: the more people who need energy, the greater the pressure on the environment.

GREEN AWARENESS There is however an encouraging difference in the growth of these new global economies to the development of the Western economy. Countries such as China started to grow while aware of the alarming effects of pollution. There has therefore been a focus on green policymaking since the beginning. There has been a lot of investment into clean energy through solar panels and wind turbines. For example, China is working on an efficient state-of-the-art distribution network for electricity, which will connect all parts of the country.

NOT A THREAT BUT RATHER AN OPPORTUNITY I am convinced that we shouldn't necessarily see the economic growth of these countries as a threat to our economy and to the earth. There are a lot of interesting opportunities for Western companies to cooperate with these new global economies. We are always one step ahead, thanks to the green technology and sustainable methods that we are developing here. The West doesn't need to passively and anxiously watch the economies of countries like Brazil and China grow. We must make a contribution using the knowledge we have gained in recent decades – after all, Western technology hasn't stood still. We have everything

it takes to deal with energy in an efficient, sustainable and environmentally friendly manner. Our capacity for continuous innovation means we can make a difference!

....

We an oppose this while still working together to combat climate change.

....

WORKING TOGETHER My conclusion is that we must share our sustainable technological solutions. This is not just for the benefit of our economy, but also of our planet! Collaboration is vital. We must not see the emerging economies merely as competitors. We will certainly need to make some sacrifices in economic terms. Yet we can still provide resistance while working together to combat climate change. We have to do this because it is no longer five to twelve but two minutes from striking midnight. We won't make it without working together...

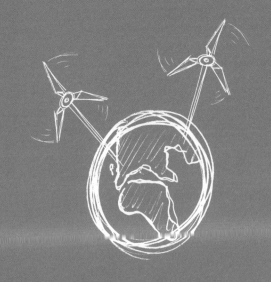

POINT OF NO RETURN?

The debate about the causes of global warming has been held and the conclusions are clear. There is an anthropogenic influence: man has caused climate change and now he is simply waiting. It seems that he needs some kind of shock in order to finally take action, yet we cannot afford to wait any longer. We should also have the courage to ask ourselves whether a turnaround is still possible, because we may already be too late ...

We may already be too late...

Delayed effects An increase in CO_2 concentration does not immediately cause a rise in temperatures. It takes thirty to fifty years for the earth to respond. The higher temperatures that we are experiencing now are thus caused by greenhouse gas emissions from the sixties and seventies. What if we stop the production of CO_2 today? Then, in thirty years time, nearly half of the carbon dioxide currently in the atmosphere will have disappeared thanks to CO_2 absorption by plants, trees and oceans, but ... the other half will remain. In short, even if we don't emit any more greenhouse gases now, temperatures will still rise by a degree. And we will suffer the consequences.

Maintaining the status quo The painful reality is that the only thing we can do is retain the status quo. And we must stop burning materials and consuming energy as if we have access to a bottomless pit. Turning the clock back is impossible, but I am 100 per cent convinced that there is an essential step that we need to take today: we need to stop consistently choosing the easiest solution with the highest return. We must not only think in the short term.

Taking the lessons we have learnt into the future We have made the transition from industrialisation to a knowledge economy. In hindsight, the reverse would obviously have been better. We made big mistakes during the Industrial Revolution, probably due to the fact that we did not know any better. Now, for the first time, we have to face up to the impact we have had on the earth. And we must learn from that by taking the good we have developed – our technology and our extensive knowledge – with us, while throwing out the bad, our polluting production methods.

It is time for clear solutions In other words, it is time for clear and clean solutions for producing energy: solar, wind, water and geothermal energy. Our technology must continue to evolve. Not just in a financial and economic sense, but in an ecological sense. Man will have to use his innovative power in a faster and more effective way. And he has that ability, there is no doubt about it.

When it is necessary, humans are capable of much more than they ever think possible. Crisis prompts us to take action. When it emerged in the eighties that our ozone layer threatened to disappear through the excessive use of CFCs, policymakers sprang into action. And their decisiveness has had an effect *(see box, page 68)*.

This shows that our leaders are indeed able to implement effective and rapid measures and that they can cut the Gordian knot. The question is why a decisive response regarding climate change has not been forthcoming. I believe the answer is as simple as it is disappointing: pressure from industry and fear of a collapsing economy are too high right now. And the threat of climate change does not seem big enough to exceed that fear. Politicians wait and trail behind. They are no longer at the front of the pack, but rather in the trailer. They analyse the situation from there and sit looking at each other expectantly while onlookers yearn for a strong and unambiguous signal that will lead to action being taken and to a victory for all of us.

Successive climate change conferences have been trying to reverse the tide *(see box, page 70)*. But measures are often half-hearted because they reflect economic interests too strongly. Policymakers do not seem to be fully aware that a society that offers no security for the future will blow up its own economy.

No choice: the earth is suffering We are hemming and hawing about taking the necessary steps, but at some point we will no longer have the luxury of choice. The first, and by far the most important, reason to take action is that the earth can't cope with our urge to consume any longer. We are putting the future of our children at risk by polluting and destroying our habitat. And we should realise that if the certainty of a future disappears, total anarchy will be all that remains.

No choice: ethics are disappearing Imagine that the existence of humanity suddenly became finite. Humans would lose all sense of morality! The climate crisis threatens our planet and all facets of our lives along with it. A second important reason to take action today is that our democracy and society are at risk, because if we don't believe in sustainability, then we don't look after each other. Then it is just each man for himself. Our morality is based on our belief in the eternity of the species. Without that belief, we would have a dog-eat-dog world.

No choice: stocks are shrinking The third reason for taking this crucial step is that our supplies of fossil fuels are limited. We can already see this in the cost price of fuel. Demand increases, supply decreases and the consequences are clear: the cost of oil, coal and gas is rising. Due to this we can currently tap into new resources, because the more expensive the product, the more it costs to mine it. We have not yet completely exhausted our stocks, but the development of alternative energy sources is becoming more urgent every day. There is an infinite supply of energy from the sun, wind, water and earth. This stock never shrinks. New techniques can help us to learn how to navigate these forms of renewable energy more efficiently. The only way to guarantee the quality of life on earth is through innovation. Innovation must be constant for humanity. This is the path we should take.

IT CAN BE DONE! THE HOLE IN THE OZONE LAYER IS GETTING SMALLER.

POLICYMAKERS ARE INDEED ABLE TO PROVIDE SWIFT AND EFFECTIVE ACTION. In the late eighties, scientists discovered that chlorofluoro-carbons (CFCs) were depleting the ozone in the atmosphere. This meant that the sun's UV rays were not being filtered to the same degree. At this time, CFCs mainly came from aerosols, refrigerators and air conditioning systems. They caused ever larger holes in the ozone layer over Antarctica and the Arctic. Scientists agreed that the use of CFCs had to stop. Industry, of course, did not agree immediately. At that time, there were very few cheap alternatives.

EFFECTIVE RESPONSE Yet the world responded very effectively after finding out that there was a hole in the ozone layer. Although scientists and industrialists did not agree with each other, politicians didn't waste any time. World leaders showed leadership by simply forbidding CFCs. And that got results, because it now seems that the ozone layer has made a slight recovery.

CLIMATE CHANGE CONFERENCE: KYOTO, COPENHAGEN, DURBAN AND DOHA

KYOTO: FINALLY A PROTOCOL In Kyoto in 1997, industrialised countries agreed to reduce greenhouse gas emissions by five per cent, with regard to 1990 levels, by 2012. Rich countries had the opportunity to offset their own emissions by way of sustainable projects in developing countries. The Kyoto Protocol came into force only in 2005. That was when Canada, Russia and Japan signed it. The United States, the largest polluter, didn't sign.

COPENHAGEN: A DISAPPOINTING RESULT By 2009, it was time for additional measures to be taken and another UN Climate Change Conference was held, this time in Copenhagen. World leaders were to decide on the successor to the Kyoto Protocol and the aim was to take action to prevent the planet from warming up any further. This didn't result in a legally binding agreement. It did, however, result in a fund being established for poor countries that suffer the consequences of climate change and a target was set to limit global warming to two degrees Celsius.

I attended the climate summit in Copenhagen. Along with Jaga, I wanted to contribute to this process of creating awareness. Our Uchronia Community sailing ship, an open innovation platform, was moored in Nyhavn from 10 to 15 December. We invited those who had witnessed climate change with their own eyes to come and tell us about their experiences.

The Polar Conservation Organisation (PCO) was one of the bodies that came to talk about the social, political and economic measures that are urgently needed to protect the polar regions.

The speech that stuck with me the most was by Will Steger, known for his legendary polar expeditions during the past forty years. He is a true witness to the disastrous consequences of climate change. In 1989 and 1990, he crossed Antarctica on foot, fully aware of the unpredictable future of the area. Five years later, he led the International Arctic Project, a journey of about 4,000 kilometres across the Arctic Ocean, from Russia to Canada via the North Pole, with dog sleds and canoes. He has seen the world change substantially in recent decades, and his foundation has worked to educate children about the impact of global warming.

DURBAN: A MISSED OPPORTUNITY In December 2011, the time was ripe for the next conference. There was a relatively small turnout at this one: only a handful of government leaders attended the summit and some of them left early. A partial solution was found at the last minute.

The 190 or so countries that participated decided to extend the Kyoto Protocol by another five years. From 2015 onwards, leaders will put on their thinking caps once more to formulate the protocol's successor: a binding agreement on reducing greenhouse gas emissions for all countries. The new protocol will apply to all countries, not just industrialised countries, given that a large portion of future CO_2 emissions will be produced by emerging economies like India and Brazil. From 2020 onwards, all countries should implement this agreement so as to limit global warming to two degrees Celsius.

A climate fund was also approved at the conference. This involved 100 billion US dollars being paid to support developing countries so they can achieve their climate targets.

Because all countries showed a willingness to reach an agreement in the long term, the conference was declared a success at the last minute. But the challenges ahead are still huge. The goal of limiting global warming to two degrees Celsius is admirable, but – based on the current measures alone – also unrealistic and unachievable. The fact is that major industrial countries like the United States, China and Russia will not be inclined to sign an agreement as long as their negotiation partners are breathing down their necks. Once they notice that their industrial, social and economic opportunities are being limited, a worthy successor to the Kyoto Protocol will undoubtedly be at risk.

DOHA: MIXED RESULTS Doha was the host for the eighteenth Climate Change Conference, in December 2012. The Kyoto Protocol again took priority. The EU member states presented themselves as a united front. They expressed their desire to join forces with the other countries to reduce greenhouse gas emissions by 30% by 2020, and to extend the Kyoto Protocol until that time. To enforce their wish, the EU parliament approved a resolution to this effect in 2012.

The EU wanted to lay the foundation for a new global climate agreement in Doha, which would come into force in 2015, as well as reach concrete agreements and rules on the extension of the Kyoto Protocol and the expansion of the climate fund for developing countries. Unfortunately, the international community saw things differently.

Many developing countries and rich countries wanted to limit the extension to five years. Because big polluters such as China, India and the United States are not bound by the protocol,

Japan, Russia, Canada and New Zealand wanted to renounce an extension.

In the end a compromise was reached. The Kyoto Protocol was extended by two years (from 2013 onwards) and will serve as a guideline until 2020 when a new climate agreement will come into force. This agreement will also be binding for emerging economies such as China and Brazil. No solution was found for the expansion of the climate fund.

Met Jaga naar de Kyo

Alle Jaga Low-H2O radiatoren verminderen de CO2-pro
gemiddeld 103 kg per jaar per won'
knokkenhout een divers

o-norm?

JAGA EXHIBITION STAND, 1997

Putting the power of fire into perspective

Did fire enable evolution? This remains a complex issue. Fire has changed everything, but certainly not only in a positive sense. The ability to control fire has given us too much power. We fancy ourselves as gods. We should take the burning torch of the gods back to Mount Olympus, before we burn our entire planet. In recent centuries, we have made the earth into a volcano by constantly extracting fuel from the ground.

and burning it to produce energy. But now we must choose a purer source. It is time to stop playing god and show respect once more for our creator: nature. Let's exchange the polluting flame for a green flame: the green force. Let's go to extremes to leave the world in a better condition than we received it in. It is high time for innovation!

~~LET THE EARTH SUFFER~~
A DIFFERENT AWARENESS: BACK TO BASICS

Back to the origin We currently supply 86 per cent of our energy requirements with fossil fuels: oil (36%), coal (27%) and gas (23%). We extracted the sources of our so-called progress from the earth and this has led to conflict between civilisation and nature. Fortunately, there are sustainable alternatives available. The possibilities for innovation are on the table. We should intervene with full conviction. Science must therefore follow, rather than chase, evolution. This is only possible if we go back to our roots, back to a balance between the four basic elements: earth, water, air and fire. And to achieve that we need to reactivate the first basic value: respect for nature.

There is no planet B.

A change in awareness A change in awareness has arisen: we must think and act differently. We have been getting everything from nature, without wondering what the consequences might be. The earth has become our instrument. Our constant hunger for raw materials, energy and food mean we have become a scourge to our planet.

We have to be closer to nature once again and show respect for the earth. The bizarre thing is that, deep down, every human being realises that we need to take this step ... and yet we still don't do it. There is a separation between our hearts, minds and behaviour, which has left us estranged from nature. The individual and the economy have taken that place. The biggest problem our society is facing and the greatest threat facing our planet right now is indifference.

The expiry date of the convenience model We must prepare our brains for a future that will be much harder: more shortages, more pollution. And that is exactly where the answer lies to why we do nothing, even though we know that something needs to change: we want to preserve our material wealth and the convenience model which we are accustomed to. We accept that in doing so, we cause irrevocable damage to nature. We are apparently able to live with the fact that we are using up everything that would have been available for future generations. The idea that we have to leave a better life behind is unthinkable.

Is prosperity possible without CO2 emission? That's the question everyone is asking.

Man is aware of the seriousness of the situation, but is prepared to sit back and wait. But in fact man should learn to be satisfied with his existence in a different way.

Our fuel supplies have almost been exhausted. Man has sucked the earth dry. In another fifty years, the resources we used so greedily in recent years will be depleted. Only a drastic change of attitude and radical innovation will allow us to reduce the impact of humans on the earth.

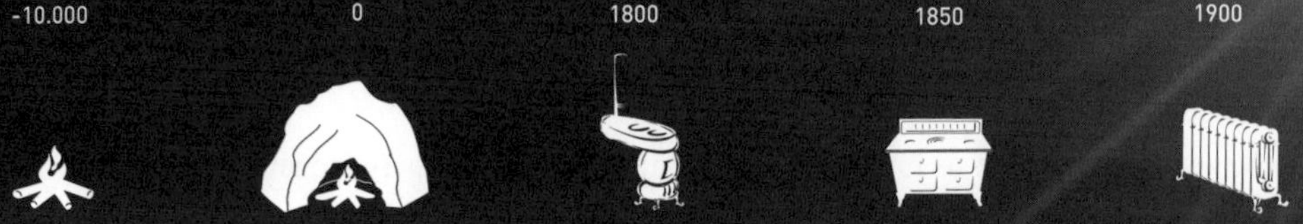

-10.000

0

1800

1850

1900

1950   1980   1995   2006   2013

We are gradually becoming aware that we are no longer able to plunder the planet with impunity.

He must appreciate the basic values of life once again, rather than being guided by legal and economic compulsions. That process of awareness is ongoing. The heyday of mass consumption is on its last legs. People are starting to look for new values, and I want to encourage them in that quest.

> *We can't turn back the clock, nor do we need to: we have the tecÚology and resources available to work in a clean and sustainable way. So what are we waiting for?*

The revolution: a new human being, a new industry

MORE EMPATHY, LESS INERTIA A revolution – that is what we need. A new human being needs to be created: one that is empathetic rather than consuming. That revolution must come from us. Everyone seems to be sitting around waiting for awareness to come from elsewhere, but this means we are losing precious time. We hide behind the system and wait passively until the decision gets made for us.

WE HAVE THE SOLUTIONS AVAILABLE TO US We used to have that sense of responsibility for the earth. We once had the urge to create added value for the generation that came after us. Industrialisation totally changed that and we can't turn back the clock. We don't need to either because technology and industry have also given us the resources to work in a clean and sustainable way. It is just that we don't use those resources enough or in the right way. Because of the large amount of oil and gas that we could have, the focus on efficiency has been pushed into the background. The first industrialists did not know any better, but we cannot use that excuse. We know that there is no longer a balance in terms of total energy. There are possibilities available for taking a collective step towards a sustainable and clean technology – I don't doubt that at all. If we all work towards the same goal, then we won't make the same mistake. And we shouldn't, because our planet can't handle that. Let's make the next Industrial Revolution green and clean!

New opportunities with new energy sources The road we need to take is one heading towards alternative energy sources. This is the only way we can create new opportunities. The earth gives us these renewable sources in the form of the four basic elements. And – just like fossil fuels – they can be found in nature. The difference is that they don't damage the earth.

FIRE: SOLAR POWER Seven days of sunlight: that is what the planet needs to meet its energy requirements for one year. Sunlight is the most powerful energy source that exists. Many scientists have already dealt with developing an efficient system to capture that energy. We now have two ways to make electricity from sunlight. The first technique is a solar boiler. It uses sunlight to heat liquid which then drives a generator. A second method is to convert sunlight directly into electricity using solar cells. The technology surrounding solar energy is continuously being improved. However, the most effective technique is undoubtedly yet to be discovered.

AIR: WIND ENERGY One month's worth of wind energy provides a full year of our planet's energy requirements. Windmills are an excellent way to generate electricity in places where the wind reaches speeds exceeding 24 kilometres per hour.

WATER: HYDROPOWER Deriving energy from water may be done by using a change in the height or the rate of flowing water. Hydropower plants generate energy from turbines or dams.

EARTH: GEOTHERMAL ENERGY Geothermal energy comes from the earth and has great potential as a sustainable energy source for the future. This type of energy is found mainly in places where the temperature below the earth's surface is high, the so-called *hot spots*, for example, on the edge of tectonic plates.

The possibilities for extracting energy from the four basic elements are endless. If we make a definitive choice for green energy, then we can really innovate. Does this pose a danger to our economy? No. On the contrary! Fossil fuels have become the easy solution. By replacing them with renewable energy sources, we can boost our creativity again, which will only serve to stimulate our economy.

LINEAR THINKING: THE WORLD AS AN INSTRUMENT
CIRCULAR THINKING: CLOSING THE MATERIAL CYCLE

Who has respect for nature, thinks in a circular manner: what goes around, comes around.

Rediscover the values of nature Respecting nature means circular thinking: seeing time and space as a circle. Those who think in straight lines see the world as an instrument. Those who think in circles realise that what goes around, comes around. This means that we need to start using healthy common sense again. The basic values that man has had for so long have been pushed into the background, along with industrialisation. We have become lazy. Idleness and comfort used to be the driving forces of evolution. If we combine our rediscovered basic values with the results of our knowledge economy – sustainable, clean technologies – we will have a world with real prospects.

Circular thinking is long-term thinking Those who think in a circular way force themselves to be patient and to let go of the desire for short-term results. They realise that everything is interconnected and that life is more than just a line with a start and an end point. Now that the earth's available reserves have nearly been exhausted, we need to close the circle of water, air, earth and fire again. That is the only way to achieve long-term thinking.

Copying nature: biomimicry The key to circular thinking comes from nature. *Biomimicry* is the term we use for the imitation of natural elements. This means nature is recognised as the creator and the basis of all life. It serves as an inspiration to solving man's problems. It is in man's character to go back to nature in times of need. It is therefore an inexhaustible source of inspiration for our human problems, because it has already devised many of the solutions that we are still diligently searching for.

One of the main examples of biomimicry that we should pursue is the elimination of waste. Nature doesn't waste. Everything in nature is reused for something else: food residues form or are the source of a new life; it is a timeless circle. We must take on this basic principle and apply it to our development process for products. The end of one product becomes the beginning of a new product. Closing our material cycles is the only way to a more sustainable way of consuming. That is how we can get the balance between man and nature back, and keep the next generation's options open.

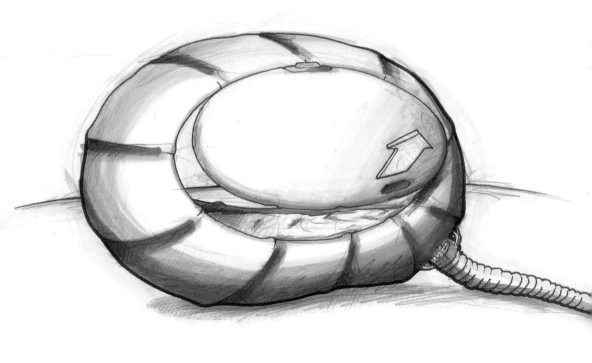

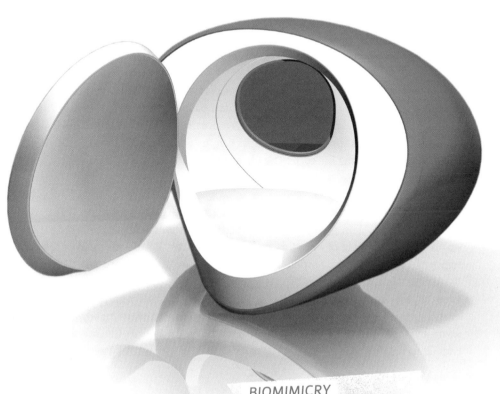

BIOMIMICRY
MOBY, MODULAR OXYGEN BUBBLE

Attention to the entire life cycle Life cycle assessment (LCA) allows us to assess the impact of a product on the environment. All life stages of the product play a role, right from raw material extraction to production, distribution, usage, maintenance, pollution and recycling. This means that LCA does not only take the role of producer into account, but also that of the end-user: the consumer.

REDUCING POLLUTION If we know the life cycle of a product, then we can determine and tackle the most polluting stages. The most damaging stage in the life of an aeroplane, for example, is its usage because so much fuel is required. The best way to reduce fuel consumption is to drastically lower the aircraft's weight and to change the way it takes off and lands. This could be done by using lighter and more durable materials. One hopeful observation is that, as science and technology evolve, products are becoming more economical and sustainable.

MORE THAN A LITERAL PRICE An LCA provides a kind of comprehensive price. It is not just the financial aspect that is decisive in price, but also the price that the environment pays for a product. Life cycle analysis makes it possible in principle to give a product a kind of pollution rating. This should be shown on the packaging along with the cost price to ensure that we are constantly aware of our impact on the environment. Price is also a relative concept. If a good becomes scarcer, then prices rise. Everything depends on availability. So you could say that the last tree on earth would be priceless. Let's hope that nobody ever needs to hang a price tag on that!

THE ULTIMATE AIM: ZERO CARBON DIOXIDE EMISSIONS By taking the life cycle of consumer goods into account, humans will start paying attention to the origin of a product again. This means that the product is more than just a thing with a direct use and a high or low cost price. We look at its origins once more. In future, efficiency should be central in the life cycle. The ultimate goal is no more CO_2 emissions: the *zero carbon economy*.

Increasingly lower potential value: from raw material to waste The current production system sees the majority of companies producing waste in the early stages. Each component of a product starts as a raw material and ends up as a useless remnant. That is entropy: a product constantly loses out in terms of quality. It loses its original value. Recycling almost always leads to entropy. The transition from white paper to recycled paper and finally newspaper ultimately always entails a clear loss in quality. We have used raw materials, energy and water ... and ultimately produced waste. In sum, we have thought about our production methods in linear rather than circular terms.

THINKING BEYOND DAMAGE LIMITATION We do not harness the full potential of our products and materials. Sustainability is higher on industry's agenda, but environmental concerns are often limited to making products less harmful. This is nowhere near enough. We must think beyond the three steps in the product's life cycle: develop, consume, and throw away. If we think in a line, then we bring everything down to a lower level. We need to think in a circle: each product is the raw material for a new product. So we choose extropy instead of entropy. We add potential to the product and close the cycle. Only then can we speak of true innovation!

START THINKING DIFFERENTLY The principle of product-to-waste dates from the Industrial Revolution. The first producers focused on practical use, efficient production and profit-making. They did not look at the bigger picture, because they assumed that the quantity of resources was infinite. The consequences are now well known, but the problem today is not that there are no possibilities for producing in another way. No, the main stumbling block is that our thinking is still dominated by eighteenth century ideas: producing and consuming as much and as fast as possible for as little expense as possible. We think that we can still use an infinite amount of resources. The result is that ecological principles are currently at the bottom of the top ten industrial concerns.

Waste becomes food

EACH PRODUCT IS RAW MATERIAL FOR A NEW PRODUCT If you want to close the material cycles, then you must assume that we have to develop products in such a way that they achieve a natural life cycle. At the end of its life cycle, a product must be the raw material for a new product, without losing out on quality. This means creating more instead of less value. Products are returned to their original value, and are the basis for the next product. If the life cycle of a product is complete then it must be degradable in nature to the maximum extent possible. It then becomes part of a new cycle.

LONGER LIFE: MODULAR DEVELOPMENT If you close the material cycles, then you need to look at consumption as well as production. It is ultimately the user of the product that determines its life cycle. This is why we need to dramatically increase product usage and prolong life cycles, allowing us to consume less overall. We need to develop products so that adjustments are possible, as soon as technology has gone one step further. This makes it unnecessary to throw away a complete product as soon as industry brings out a new model. The target is *modular production*: appliances that develop along with every stage in the life of the user.

THE CHALLENGE IS A NEW FORM OF CONSUMPTION Technical feasibility for closing the material and energy cycles is high. We have the know-how and expertise to do this at each stage of the industrial and economic process. And if we set this as a task for our creative economy, then it will only be a matter of time before new products come out. The real challenge will be to put these products on the market because restoring consumer goods has become rare nowadays. Replacing them is often easier, which has made throwing things away the norm. The solution is to make adjustments easier and to abolish mass production while taking consumers' wishes into account. Tailoring products to suit the taste of a region, or even an individual, will increase their value. Then the products won't just end up on the dump without any further thought. This is one of the main functions of the creative economy: making unique products following nature's example.

CONSUMING LESS Commitment to a mentality change is required not just by producers, but also by consumers. Humanity must not keep on consuming increasing amounts, but should rather strive to consume less. Should we go back to pre-Industrial Revolution times then? Of course not. But we do need *tempered consumption*, even if we do start using more ecologically efficient products. There is a huge temptation to consume more of a product if there is an ecological label stuck on it, even though raw materials, energy and water have also been used for that product. Handling our consumer goods in a responsible way is the main challenge for the future.

Crucial step for companies

PRODUCING AND TRANSFORMING SUSTAINABLY Modern companies that close their material cycle will be able to attain a waste-free, sustainable way of producing using clean technology. This is firstly done by reusing old materials as often as possible or by giving them a new purpose. Products that are at the end of their life cycle need to be biodegradable. This means they can become raw materials again and the cycle truly is complete. Secondly, each company needs to develop products that consumers use and reuse efficiently for as long as possible: modular production. These sustainable products continue to prove their usefulness and are therefore less likely to be thrown away.

THINKING ECONOMICALLY, ETHICALLY AND ECOLOGICALLY Companies that change their mentality and choose ecological production give equal weight to ethics and the environment and to the economy. They make better designs, develop different products and manage their own cycles, so that nature can recover. This implies a focus on diversity and effectiveness, which also takes into account future generations. These companies choose an industry and technology that enriches nature instead of damaging it.

NO WASTE, MORE EFFICIENCY It goes without saying that companies must be able to guarantee their survival in the same way organisms do. Profitability is not a nice little bonus, but rather a necessity. As an entrepreneur, I am fully aware of that. I am convinced that companies that close or self-manage their material and energy cycles, can expect a higher return. They don't just create greater ecological value, but also create a more profitable path in commercial terms by bringing products onto the market which offer today's consumers a better standard of living in times of a future lack of materials. In a society that is re-attaching importance to sustainability, this is the way of doing business in the future. Attention must therefore be focused on fulfilling needs in new business models, not attaining higher production and consumption figures.

DON'T JUST WAIT – TAKE ACTION At Jaga, I have always tried to reduce the impact of our products on nature and the results have been a success, both ecologically and economically. We have done that by developing new technologies and constantly improving existing products *(see box, page 90)*.

I believe managers have a duty to introduce the appropriate expertise into their companies. The brains to make efficient, beautiful and ecologically sound products already exist in many companies, but are not used enough, or at all. Entrepreneurs cannot wait for decisive politicians to take action. *They* must be the basis of change. Let them lead the pack while the world waits for decisive leaders to emerge. Perhaps these entrepreneurs can inspire politicians to sail along with them and eventually take the helm.

THE JAGA METHOD: INCREASINGLY MORE ECONOMICAL AND EFFICIENT

The difference between the heavy cast iron radiators of 1900 and the devices you see today in modern homes is huge – not just in terms of appearance, but also in economy and efficiency. The volume of water in old radiators was enormous. At the beginning of the twentieth century, 100 litres of water was needed to heat a relatively small space. Several kilos of steel had to be heated up, which wasted a lot of energy and materials. In short: these were an inefficient and environmentally destructive way of producing heat.

LESS WATER, LESS VOLUME In the eighties, Jaga developed the Low H_2O technology: radiators with limited water content. The amount of water in the apparatus was drastically reduced. The radiators themselves became lighter and more compact which meant they were more efficient than traditional radiators. Working with universities, Jaga went looking for the most efficient ratio between water volume and the surface area to be heated. This was how Jaga was able to create a desirable product in times of crisis. Reaction times were optimised: if enough free heat was available – in the form of sunlight and body heat – then the unit turned itself off. By taking away the issue of double heating, the consumer wasted a lot less energy. Those who installed Low H_2O radiators in their homes were able to reduce annual CO_2 emissions by 100 kilograms per radiator because they used 12 per cent less energy.

LESS LOSS OF HEAT: LOW SURFACE TEMPERATURE The great revolution was that new Jaga radiators no longer radiated any excessive heat. It was not the radiator that was being heated, but rather the air in the room. The Low Surface Temperature radiator did just what the name suggests: however hot the water that ran through the tubes and unit became, the radiator was never warmer than 40 degrees Celsius. The benefits were endless: the radiators were safer to touch,

because they were not as hot; energy wasn't being lost through the walls behind the radiator, so the device could also stand in front of a glass wall without any risk of breakage. The radiator became even more efficient when Jaga started making temperature control equipment: the first ultrafast thermostats made temperature control in the home easier and more economical. This a fairly common product now, but then it was a pioneering invention …

SUSTAINABLE MATERIALS At the start of the twenty-first century, Jaga created the first radiator in wood: *Knockonwood*. This is a durable product that combines low energy usage with optimum heat dissipation. *Knockonwood* received the quality label of the Forest Stewardship Council, an organisation that wants to tackle reckless timber extraction. On top of that, Jaga planted a Robinia tree in the Jaga forest for every radiator of this type that was sold. These trees absorb a lot of CO_2.

SUPER-FAST HEATING: DYNAMIC BOOST EFFECT A new technology – the Dynamic Boost Effect (DBE) – made Jaga radiators even more effective and more energy efficient. Boosters increased the thermal efficiency of the Low H_2O heat exchanger by 250 per cent using the same material. The system made radiators much more powerful, meaning they could be much smaller. A space was heated up to nine times faster. DBE is the fastest and most economical heating system in the world and is suitable for alternative energy and low temperatures. Jaga launched the innovative technology in a special way. During the Boost Party, hundreds of visitors were given a spectacular demonstration (see also page 153).

DARING TO THINK AHEAD Thirty years ago, Jaga was prepared for the ecological problems that our world is currently facing. At that time, Jaga was already aware of the need for energy and material

....

Our job is to make radiators people don't know yet ...

....

efficiency. The consumption of the product during its usage phase was minimised and its development was extremely sustainable. Dreaming, thinking ahead and daring to give things a go ... for me, that is where true innovation lies.

ENERGY-EFFICIENT LOW TEMPERATURE INSTALLATION
45°C supply temperature, 35°C return temperature, 20°C indoor temperature , - 10 degrees outdoor temperature

45/35/20 ΔT = 20 K	FLOOR HEATING *		RADIATORS		JAGA RADIATORS	
	WET SYSTEM	DRY SYSTEM	CAST IRON	STEEL PANEL	LOW-H20	DBE BOOST
H L (mm) D	6.5 cm concrete 51m²	2 cm concrete 51m²	1000x 2600x 250	900x 2250x 200	700x 2200x 220	400x 1200x 170
Water (kg)	57	57	122	39	6	2
Weight (kg) **	6143	2743	238	178	16	6
Total (kg)	6200	2800	360	217	22	8
Power (W) in confort for DBE	2000	2000	2000	2000	2000	2000
Heat storage (Wh)	7000	3200	3500	1500	190	80
Material Efficiency W/kg (mPt)	0,32	0,71	5,5	9	91	250
LCA score ***(mPt)	248 700	184 100	248 744	185 853	123 400	49 780
Recycling (mPt)	0	0	- 82 915	- 61 951	- 22 172	
Gas m³ to heat up	4	2	2	1	0,1	0,05
Heating time	very slow	very slow	slow	average	fast	very fast

*24°C on floorsurface / ** weight heating element / *** According to the Ovam ecolizer database 1.0 (www.ovam.be)
(mPt) = Millipoints

JAGA MINI CANAL
LOW-H2O TECHNOLOGY

TRUE BEAUTY COMES FROM WITHIN
JAGA LOW H2O + DYNAMIC BOOST EFFECT
250% MORE POWER / 9x FASTER

JAGA KNOCKONWOOD FREESTANDING DBE
"LIVING TOMORROW" VILVOORDE, BELGIUM

THOUGHTLESS ENERGY CONSUMPTION
SELF-SUFFICIENCY AS AN OPTIMAL GREEN SOLUTION

*Self-sufficiency is the most
sustainable solution. It is
a return to nature, to the
origins of life.*

The mentality change that I have deliberately chosen
for this first basic value – *Respect Nature* – makes the
next step in our path towards a sustainable way of life
obvious. Because if we take into account the life cycle
of products and try to close the material cycle, then we
come naturally to the best solution: self-sufficiency.

Self-sufficiency means getting back to our origins and
trying to imitate nature. Fauna and flora have always provided for their own basic
needs. This makes the tree the ultimate symbol of efficiency.

The tree: the power of nature

THE TREE FEEDS ITSELF AND ITS SURROUNDINGS The tree gets everything it needs to
live from its immediate surroundings. It extracts water and nutrients from the soil,
but the majority of its biomass comes from the carbon dioxide that it extracts from
the air. Thanks to chloroplasts, its leaves use light and carbon dioxide to form glucose
and its roots absorb water, oxygen and nutrients from the soil. This creates the carbohydrates that it needs to grow and to form its leaves and buds.

Yet trees don't work on this process of photosynthesis just for themselves. They create
the oxygen that people and animals need to be able to breathe, and they reduce the
amount of carbon dioxide in the air. Trees also contribute to nature in many other
ways: birds build their nests; algae, moss and fungi grow on trunks and branches; and
insects live on the leaves of a tree while squirrels and birds feast on the fruit.

Special vitality The vitality of trees is particularly impressive. If the main trunk of
a tree is severely damaged, then one of the branches can keep growing to become the
dominant branch. This means trees can survive for many hundreds, even thousands,
of years. They symbolise the power of nature and it is therefore unsurprising that they
are sacred icons all over the world.

In short, a tree doesn't just provide for all its own basic needs, it also contributes to the
life of others. Its way of life stands in stark contrast to the way man deals with energy.
Whereas the tree is an example of extropy, humans are heading in the direction of
entropy: decay. Instead of operating in a more energy-efficient way, humans are looking farther and farther afield for sources of energy. This means they need to consume
more and more to achieve the same effect.

JAGA "BOOST INTO THE FUTURE" STAND
BATIBOUW 2012 - BRUSSELS, BELGIUM

From entropy to extropy

As humans, we should be just as effective at coping with energy as a tree is. If we close the circle and are able to completely provide for our own basic needs, then we do not constantly lose more value. Instead, we become more efficient, and that is good for us and for nature. Self-sufficiency means we restore the natural balance and slowly return to the earth's former state.

An individual energy field for each person We have the technology available to enable us to be self-sufficient. The combination of solar panels and heat pumps means every person can fully meet his own energy needs. Just like the tree, he doesn't just wait for energy to come to him, but creates it himself. He doesn't draw his strength from the energy reserves of the past, but from the present, and in such a way that the planet is not affected at all. Clean technology is *the* way to a clean future.

This system of self-sufficiency is therefore nothing but advantageous. The earth benefits from this and, if that is not enough for you, so do you. If you are no longer dependent on the fluctuating energy and material prices in an uncertain market, you can give yourself enormous amounts of freedom. And you can retrieve additional returns from the system because you can share or sell the energy you do not need to others. The line between producers, consumers and suppliers becomes very thin.

When I envision the future, I imagine that this way of life is possible for every inhabitant of the earth. Using self-sufficiency and clean technology, we can create a *universal* survival model.

THE ARCHETYPE FOR RESPECT NATURE:
THE GREEN ENGINEER

There is an archetype for each of the five basic values; a type of person that every society and business needs to create that value. The awareness of each value should be present in all of us.

The engineer plays an important role in the search for a universal survival model. He has the knowledge that humanity needs to live differently, but the engineer we needs to help shape our future cannot be the same kind of engineer as the one that set the Industrial Revolution in motion.

Like the engineers of the eighteenth and nineteenth century, the current generation of engineers is still predominantly Cartesian. They see development and production as a linear one-way model. They focus on a problem and try to solve it in a serial manner. The easiest and cheapest solution will be given preference. A high return in the short term is key.

The engineers and ingenious minds of today must learn to think in a circular fashion once more. They must observe natural processes and use nature as an example. In other words, they need to see the world in a more holistic, organic and empathic way. By taking into account the life cycle of the products they develop, they can strive to attain a broader form of efficiency – not just in economic terms, but also ecologically.

It is high time that engineers put clean technology first. Other forms of technology should be a thing of the past. These do not solve problems, they only serve to exacerbate current problems. They do not provide any kind of innovation or progress.

Collaboration between engineers and creative minds is crucial for making the most essential step towards innovation. The future lies in individual products for individual consumers, not in mass production and mass consumption. Products that have been given a soul are automatically more sustainable. The engineer needs the Artist's help to give the product that soul. The second value – *Awake the Artist* – articulates the importance of creativity in innovation.

VALUE 2

AWAKE
THE ARTIST

VALUE 2

The creativity of man knows no bounds. In an artistic society, consumers avoid the path of mass consumption. Companies choose wholeheartedly to create value by way of creativity and developing innovative materials and production tecÚiques. They make the transition from pure design to art. Society follows and chooses a creative economy that gives the planet a new chance.

THE
BEATEN
PATH

AWAKE
THE ARTIST

THE CURSE OF MASS CONSUMPTION

Mass production, mass distribution, mass consumption. The Industrial Revolution created countless new opportunities with few or no restrictions. In the middle of the eighteenth century, producing similar products on a large scale was very labour intensive. But from the moment that machines could take over the work of a human being, a radical change came about. After all, a machine could spit out 20 or 2,000 products ... If the demand was there, the supply was simply increased.

The consequences of this mass consumption can be felt on several fronts. It is not just our earth that is suffering – although it does seem to be the biggest victim right now. The impact on our society and the identity of the individual is also immense. Man, and his environment, have changed fundamentally due to our increasing consumerism.

Without artistic input, alienation ensues. Mass consumption is synonymous with soulless products.

Landfill earth Man's consumption habits since about two centuries ago have really put our planet under pressure. The World Wildlife Fund has calculated that the world consumed 20 per cent more natural resources ten years ago than the planet can reproduce itself. The consequences can be clearly felt: forests are disappearing, natural resources are diminishing, and species are dying out.

The earth gets our waste in exchange for its natural resources. Now there is an unfair bargain, if ever there was one! Because we have so many options, we throw away products as quickly and as recklessly as we buy them. Brands or gadgets lose their status and trends change quickly, so we throw products away and replace them with something new. And the landfills are expanding. The plastic archipelago in the Pacific is just one example of the shocking consequences of this behaviour (*see box, page 112*).

Moreover (and by now I really shouldn't need to remind you of this) it is the countries that consume the least that are most affected by over-consumption. Rising sea levels, more intense rainfall, loss of agricultural land ... these are problems that mainly affect the poorer regions in the south, even though the ecological footprint of people from those countries is much lower than that of countries for which mass consumption has become a way of life in recent centuries.

Society of alienation The importance of status and possession in today's society is increasing. The car you drive, the clothes you wear, the house you live in ... all are considered to be reflections of who we are and who we want to be. Consumption gives us an identity. This results in a vicious circle, because if everyone around us has more resources and therefore a higher status, *we* need to keep consuming more and more to reach a higher status. We keep on bidding against each other.

Those who want to consume need to earn more. And this is often synonymous with working long hours and climbing the career ladder as fast as possible. The increased workload associated with this has an ever-increasing impact on our society. Achieving material wealth is given priority over contact with family, friends, neighbours ... Little by little, we are distancing ourselves from our surroundings. The spasmodic way in which we try to collect as many friends as possible through social media sites can hardly serve to offset that.

Individuals looking for values This alienation of society is strongly linked to another consequence of mass consumption: fewer and fewer people link their identity to religion, philosophy or cultural traditions. The choice we made during the Industrial Revolution – work and produce more rather than make room for self-development – has been decisive in this. For a lot of people, consumption has taken the place of religion and tradition. Our self-esteem is closely linked to what we have; what we have is who we are. Consumption is linked to our personal happiness.

Increasing consumerism has alienated us from our true desires. We seem to be constantly looking for things to make us happy, and we always think we can get that from material objects. Our deeper, intangible needs have been pushed further into the background, meaning that we often no longer recognise ourselves.

A world without diversity As a result of industrialisation and mass consumption, the uniqueness and diversity of many cultures have been lost. While travelling, I have been able to see the world change dramatically with my very own eyes. Villages that I visited thirty years ago have become huge cities and, whereas continents and regions used to be so different, everything has started to look the same. This is particularly evident in certain parts of Asia. A city like Shanghai was once a village. Now it is a metropolis dominated by skyscrapers, neon signs and cars. Industrialisation has made everything look the same and variety has disappeared. When you landed at an airport in the past, you were immediately immersed in a new culture. Today airports look the same – that picturesque individuality gone. It doesn't matter whether you're landing in Mexico City or Kuala Lumpur, the impact of culture has disappeared.

Mass consumption kills creativity Modern people buy things. They need something, so they go to the shop, make their choice from a huge and endless range of products, and then return home. Their needs are satisfied – but only for a while, as pure consumption does not give rise to long-term satisfaction. Nowadays we rarely make or create something ourselves – buying is much easier. It seems that our creativity is threatened with extinction.

TECHNOLOGY AS A NEW GOD

Who knows exactly what's behind the devices we use every day? Our tecÚical knowledge is no longer sufficient for understanding how something works.

Our attitude toward technology has changed under the influence of excessive consumption. In our modern society, technology has turned into a kind of omnipotent god. We would never have come this far without it. The result is a collection of intangible artefacts which – at first sight – appear to make our lives easier. But nobody knows exactly what is behind either small devices or the large machinery that we use. This has caused a serious deterioration in our technical knowledge. We barely know how things we use every day work.

TecÚology hides our energy consumption Man has almost always hidden technological processes. Our devices are designed in such a way as to conceal how they operate. But this also makes consumption – the flame behind the technology – invisible. We don't see what is responsible for creating energy. And we can easily ignore the fact that essentially every device is an energy conversion system. Awareness of the impact that everyday objects have on nature has therefore largely disappeared, despite the fact that we are constantly burning a huge flame on our planet.

Of course, technology has formed the basis of many aspects of progress. And as the manager of an innovative company, you cannot be averse to technology. On the contrary, you should consider technology to be the only path to a sustainable future. My childhood didn't just revolve around nature – technology was ubiquitous too. My father installed central heating and, as a child, I was allowed to help him weld pipes and do all sorts of other chores in his workshop. I also tested my homemade radiators there. It intrigued me to discover how systems fit together. I always wanted to know exactly how a device worked. This childlike fascination resurfaced when I started working at Jaga because the urge to learn never left me. That kind of curiosity in the field of technology can be a great revelation for each child.

TecÚology restricts creativity Technology has removed the need for creativity for many people. It has made us lazy – sent us to sleep. Everyday activities require less and less thought, which is disastrous for the way we operate. The only thing we seem capable of doing is choosing; creating or producing things ourselves has become a rarity. Rekindling this creativity will be one of the main challenges for a sustainable future.

THE END OF CREATIVITY?

The Industrial Revolution gave rise to a society of un-precedented technological applications and unbridled consumption. Creativity – which every man possesses – slowly slipped away. We can still catch a glimpse of it in our children and that basic creativity can still be seen in countries where over-consumption is not yet the norm. These examples can provide us with the in-spiration for a new way of living and working.

....

Mass consumption and tecÚology are killing off our creativity.

....

The uninhibited spirit of a child

IMAGINARY POWER AND OPENNESS   Children have free minds; they are artists. They are uninhibited and their thought patterns have not yet been fixed. A child who is given a birthday gift but casts its contents aside to play with the wrapping paper is letting his or her imagination run wild. A child who lives in imaginary worlds has an ability which an adult can only envy, for it is that openness that we need to put our creative minds back to work.

During that peak of creativity – your childhood – your environment is decisive in your thinking later in life. This was also true for me. All the ingredients for my later philosophical beliefs and business ideas were already present during my childhood. They were inherent in my family of opposites and the unique surroundings in which I grew up.

A MIXTURE OF CREATIVE INFLUENCES   My mother came from a rather creative and philosophical background in which aesthetics were the great ideal. At family gath-erings, I listened to lofty discussions and wonderful speeches. Challenging the bourgeoisie with creativity and a desire for freedom became a subtle game during my youth. But it was my mother's brother who was an inspiring figure, artistically speaking. He sparked my interest in philosophy and anthropology. He didn't work, but rather philosophised, wrote, composed and mused on subjects such as art, music, spirituality and the cosmos. He introduced me to topics, which I would then enthusi-astically go and learn about. As a child, I stuck to reading and dreaming, but as soon as I could, I went out to discover the world.

My father, on the other hand, came from a very different family. A work ethic – getting things done – was paramount. He was an unusually hard worker from an agricul-tural family who did everything himself, and was technically very skilled. He created a home environment for us in which there was room for nature and technology. I was allowed to keep birds and experiment with breeding new species. These ornamental

PLASTIC SOUP

Mass consumption has profound implications for our environment. One of the many tragic examples of extensive water pollution is the so-called *plastic archipelago* in the Pacific. If you haven't heard of it, then the term 'plastic soup' should clarify the concept for you. There are huge amounts of waste – plastic in particular – which float around in the north Pacific Ocean. This is mainly due to a large annular sea current, which gathers the waste and makes it collect in one spot. The exact dimensions of the archipelago are still being discussed: scientists have estimated anything from one to 15 million square kilometres.

The plastic particles are so small that jellyfish and fish can eat them. The consequences of this are not just significant for life in the ocean, but also for the birds that eat the fish. Pollution of the wa-

ter has affected entire ecosystems, as well as biodiversity. The impact on our health, society and economy is severe.

A few years ago, I wanted to show Jaga employees the madness of this human-based impact on nature. I did this in a very confrontational way. I left a unique masterpiece by Dirk Claesen from Zephyr at the factory door: a dead sperm whale. These animals live in all of our oceans and have lived on earth for millions of years. They have survived just about every disaster that has befallen the planet, and yet they are dying off due to plastic pollution in our seas. I wanted to make everyone aware of this. Was this confrontational? Yes, but I got my message across.

chickens walked around both inside and outside at home; they laid eggs in the flower-pots. We made our own go-carts with the engines of discarded lawn-mowers. That was how – in a very different way – my father created the perfect breeding ground for my creativity and my understanding of science and technology.

BROADMINDEDNESS AS A SOURCE OF INNOVATION In short, a child is open to different views and approaches, which may seem too extreme at first glance. But those who want to be innovative must go and look for that unique openness, that open-minded perspective, that admiration you felt as a child when looking at a globe, running after self-bred animals in the garden, driving a homemade go-cart or listening to an eccentric uncle.

Creative cultures

MAKE IT YOURSELF Creativity is still widespread in many non-Western countries. People who do not (and cannot) rely on simply buying things are forced to use their minds, and the resources they have available to them, to find solutions. They create things themselves. Compare that to a Western society where all the products and services we buy are ready-made. The need for creativity seems to have disappeared.

SELF-RELIANCE During my travels to countries like Poland, the Czech Republic, Lithuania, Russia, Bulgaria and China, I noticed that the people there are still creative. They are more independent, which they had to be during communism. They haven't lost that self-reliance and are capable of profound creativity and perseverance. They are often aware of the technology behind the products they are using. They fix things that break themselves. Exactly the opposite of the West: we are much more dependent on companies, institutions, organisations and services. We buy finished products and when something breaks, we replace it with something new.

CREATING THINGS YOURSELF IS INNOVATING Can we only rediscover our creativity by living like these people? Of course not. Although the chances are that we *will* have to give up certain comforts because of a scarcity of resources. We must start preparing ourselves for this new future now, by getting rid of our laziness and starting to provide for our own basic needs again. Only then can we truly innovate.

CRISIS AS A TRIGGER FOR CREATIVITY

The first decade of the twenty-first century was dominated by the global climate crisis and subsequent economic crises. Now we are at a threshold: we are slowly becoming aware that a certain form of luxury will disappear. Negativity and fear are dominant now. Yet we are being given a unique opportunity: there is room for creativity again.

Crisis necessitates innovation Nothing is as deadly to the creative human spirit as the immediate fulfilment of our needs. When everything's going well, people are conservative. They see no need to change something that has already shown itself to be useful. But a crisis forces them to look for solutions which may – and should – be creative. Repeating the same method is not an option. If we lose our comfort we will need to look for creative alternatives out of sheer necessity.

As long as everything's going well, people are quite conservative. But in times of crisis, they are forced to tread other, more creative, paths.

Innovation means thinking ahead When I got involved in the family business during the oil crisis, I found myself at a crossroads, with conservatism to one side and the necessity to innovate to the other. I had returned to Belgium after many years of travelling around the world. It was an exceptionally difficult period, economically speaking, but that crisis turned out to be a blessing because people were more open to innovation. Jaga chose to pursue sustainability and began developing heat pumps. By making energy from outside air, Jaga was more economical and polluted less. And although the economy was at a particularly low ebb, the product was a success. The technology of heat pumps was still in its infancy, but Jaga was already applying the technique in thousands of homes. After the oil crisis, the price of fossil fuels plummeted again, and everyone switched back to less technologically advanced, more environmentally *un*friendly energy sources. But a few decades later, the attention to ecologically sound solutions and energy efficiency has never been greater. My conclusion is that innovation means thinking ahead – even if the market is not quite ready for it.

HEATWAVE BY JAGA & JORIS LAARMAN
PLAYFUL CURLS MADE FROM A CONCRETE SHELL

AWAKE
THE ARTIST

THE
PATH
OF
INNOVATION

Creative innovation requires a drastic change in attitudes and an accelerated awareness of individual consumers, businesses and society in general.

~~THE CURSE OF MASS CONSUMPTION~~
THE NEW CONSUMER

Looking for a different way to consume The difference between today's consumers and those of several decades ago is huge. Standard products don't interest us any more. We are looking for unique items, products that highlight our personality. We want to distinguish ourselves by choosing objects that have meaning. The growing success of products that allow us to make things ourselves shows that the way we consume has altered significantly.

Art and creativity provide an effective alternative for mass consumption. Those who create choose a different sense of identity. And that effect is not just achievable through music, theatre, literature, photography or painting. By thinking about the development process and product design, we avoid the path of mass production. This helps us to stimulate human creativity once more.

Art, creativity and design offer an effective alternative for mass consumption.

Happiness lies in creativity
ART MAKES ALL THE DIFFERENCE My first value – *Respect Nature* – showed that man must live in balance with nature. That is an absolute prerequisite. But it is not just balance that brings people happiness. Creativity creates a higher consciousness: creating helps you get to know yourself. Art can make a difference in daily life because it affects our moods and actions, and also determines how we think about our time here on earth. By creating things, by making something with the resources available to us, we open up prospects for the future and innovate for ourselves.

If someone gets the opportunity to be creative, he is happy.

CREATING MAKES US HAPPIER Creating brings satisfaction and happiness. The joy of buying cannot compare to this because buying is an automatic process that doesn't require a creative mind. In an economy where everything is provided ready-made, we are repeatedly prompted to pursue immediate satisfaction. This means we have to deal with the law of diminishing value: we need more and more objects in order to feel that same sense of satisfaction.

However, a creative person experiences a feeling that consumption can never bring about. I am convinced that creativity could help to make people in Western countries happier again. Being creative is a basic value that every human being possesses and we need to regain that if we want to combat alienation. Let's reawake the artist within every individual! By doing something ourselves, we feel unique. The path to your own creation is much more valuable than the path to the shops.

The ultimate creative challenge: self-sufficiency Until a few decades ago, we could make most things we used ourselves. We had great creative abilities, which kept us close to nature. Nowadays our creative participation is almost non-existent. We don't participate in the development of the products we need in everyday life any more. Making something instead of buying it should be our new reflex. In this way, we encourage diversity rather than constantly slowing it down and oppressing it.

FROM ENTROPY TO EXTROPY I have already cited the example earlier in this book: the simple pot of yoghurt that we eat for breakfast. It contains about 80 kilocalories and provides about an hour's worth of energy, yet man has used at least 10 times as much energy to produce, package and transport this yoghurt. This reasoning is true for almost every product we use: it costs more energy than it yields. And the fact that we import our products from all parts of the globe uses a lot of energy. The transition from entropy to extropy is one that needs to be made urgently. This is the only way we can limit the impact of our consumption on the earth. To make this necessary transition, we must reactivate our creativity.

DECENTRALISATION VERSUS GLOBAL ECONOMY Partial decentralisation is our future: wherever possible, we should make things ourselves. The global economy is not doomed – the distance we've covered is too far for that to happen. But we must gradually evolve into a system of self-sufficiency. In the future, those who build their own houses, provide their own food and make as many objects as possible themselves, will be in a stronger position. Self-sufficiency is central to the universal survival model which we are eagerly looking for today.

SELF-SUFFICIENCY: IMPOSED OR CHOSEN? Self-sufficiency requires a great deal of creativity and expertise, yet those who choose to take this path will guarantee themselves a stronger position in society. The feeling of powerlessness that we unconsciously associate with having or wanting to buy everything, will disappear. In this respect, creativity is the precise opposite of consumption. Those who know how

JAGA TWINE
CREATE YOUR OWN @ MILANO MOBILE 2011

CREATE YOUR OWN
SPHINX FACTORY - MAASTRICHT, THE NETHERLANDS

products work and who can develop and repair things themselves are able to limit pure consumption to an absolute minimum.

What will happen if we don't make this move towards self-sufficiency? The answer is simple: it will undoubtedly be imposed on us from outside. If our supply of fossil fuels becomes more scarce and we have not developed enough alternatives, then the global economy will be finished and every society will invert into itself out of necessity.

~~TECHNOLOGY AS THE NEW GOD~~
CREATIVITY AS A BASIS FOR BUSINESS

We need to create a global platform that will provide the impetus for a different economy, which doesn't just revolve around financial gain. We must reconcile the economy with values and spirituality so that creativity becomes the engine of the economy. Because right now we are far too concerned with numbers.

Space for creativity and dreaming Creativity requires space to experiment. In business, employees can only take that step if there is an open and free culture in which they are challenged to go off the beaten track in their thoughts and actions, and in which people don't anxiously protect their newly acquired knowledge or positions.

INNOVATION MEANS DARING TO IMAGINE We need to reserve a place for dreams once again. Innovation means fuelling passion and daring to dream. This is a difficult task because dreams belong to a culture, which meets resistance from most entrepreneurs. Our current economy is mostly based on short-term successes and securities. Investments should immediately produce a profit and be as transparent as possible. In an economy like this, an employee who dreams and who achieves non-quantifiable results through trial and error is a risk. Because what if his dreams don't lead to an immediate return?

A NEW MINDSET To allow companies to make the transition to a more creative and innovative approach, there has to be a radical change of mentality. Most businesses sweep the most difficult issues under the carpet. They look for averages and cling to what they have. But we have to dare to walk away from traditions and generalities. We have to simulate a situation in which the things we have today are not around any more.

BEING CREATIVE IN A PRODUCTIVE WAY Entrepreneurs often assume that creativity is a wild leap into the dark, but this is not the case. Creativity is a very specific jump to clear values in society and leads to innovation and progress. Creativity requires freedom, flexibility, courage and tolerance. Entrepreneurs need to bring these elements into their businesses. This is the only way that they can take on the challenge to make creativity economically viable.

CREATIVITY WITH A PURPOSE We can integrate art into our economy by making it productive. Creativity has a clear goal in a creative economy: innovation and sustainability. Art for art's sake, purely for the development of the soul, seems pointless to me. The creativity I'm talking about, however, is a lever for the spirit; it also serves social and material purposes. It creates something structural for people in their surroundings and makes a change to our way of thinking.

ROOM FOR ARTISTS IN THE WORLD OF BUSINESS Those who want to innovate need to provide a place for artists and dreamers in their companies. They need to create a culture of tolerance in terms of diversity by encouraging rather than discouraging differences. This idea is often met with resistance in the type of economy we have today. Dreamers and creative people are difficult for economists to manage, as the latter rely on 'harsh reality' and the certainty of figures. The ability to innovate therefore lies in bringing these different types of people together into a kind of free zone where they can work on a creative philosophy. The conflicts that arise between artists, engineers and economists give rise to functional, beautiful and sustainable designs. If your company does not provide this kind of opportunity to its employees, then you can never really develop special products.

ECONOMIC GROWTH REQUIRES FREEDOM Richard Florida, an American sociologist, expresses this idea perfectly. He says the fastest growing economy is the one in which there is the most freedom. I agree: to run a successful business, you need to employ all archetypes and you have to give them complete freedom to work together. You need to create a group of people which is as heterogeneous as possible. This requires a change in mindset because people naturally prefer to surround themselves with those who are like-minded.

INNOVATION BY BURNING A lot of people – and a lot of businesses – need to make a *tabula rasa*. They must wipe the slate clean and start all over again; burn down everything and start all over again. Those who cling onto the same values will not be able to evolve.

Creativity is the attitude of trying everything you can imagine. So don't assume that something can or cannot be done ... *try* it. Keep striving for the ultimate goal. To achieve really sustainable ideas, you need to test a thousand and one things by starting from scratch. A creative economy allows this because it sets people in motion and gives them the space to try things out, as well as to fail and start all over again.

JAGA PLAY

Prosumption: products with a soul Deciding to make a purchase is not just a rational decision, but also an emotional one. Consumers are more aware of what they are buying today because they realise that we are living in a time of scarcity. They incorporate ecological and ethical factors into their buying behaviour. The entrepreneur who realises this will be able to follow the right course in terms of innovation.

We don't just heat up your home but also your soul.

A HUMAN BEING IS MORE THAN A CONSUMER In my view, companies should not see people just as consumers. Consumption kills creativity so we must look at the soul again, and start creating together. As companies, we should not take creative power away from people. The solution lies in participatory creativity and open innovation.

DEVELOPING AND PRODUCING TOGETHER Let consumers take part in the development process of the products they are buying, because that's where the future lies. In one word: *prosumption*. The term comes from Alvin Toffler *(see box, page 130)*. He added the 'pro' from proactive to the 'sumption' of consumption. According to Toffler, consumers can play an active role in the improvement or development of products and services. In a market that is saturated by mass production, he believes that the role of the consumer is no longer that of a passive, indifferent buyer of products. It sounds like a relatively young and innovative idea, but it's more than thirty years old. I took his book *The Third Wave* with me during my trips around the world in the eighties. His progressive ideas have shaped my own and inspired me on several levels.

INTERACTION WITH PLAY The radiator *Play* is Jaga's example of the creative 'prosumer' approach. This radiator allowed me to combine two basic values: *Respect Nature*, as the radiator uses the famous Low H_2O technology and is made from organic, sustainable materials, and *Awake the Artist*, as the customer was able to choose from a wide variety of shapes and colours for the casing with rounded corners. The valve was fully integrated into the design. The radiator was a great success, thanks to the freedom that customers were given to participate in the design.

A THOUGHTFUL SELECTION OF UNIQUE PRODUCTS I never believed in the doctrine that individual products for individual consumers are not profitable. Look at nature: everything is unique. And would you say that nature is unprofitable? Very early in my career at Jaga, I became convinced that products that have meaning for their owner take on an added value, which makes them more durable and more valuable. My views were confirmed: people have more and more of an urge to *experience* rather than to consume. By buying products with a personal meaning, we feel unique. This philosophy took shape at Jaga both in exhibition stands *(see box, page 133)* and in the establishment of the Jaga Experience Lab, a place where all our technical, economic and creative minds can come together *(see box, page 137)*.

Another perspective on design

UNIVERSAL BEAUTY   Universal beauty exists. The things that a Westerner likes can often be appreciated by an African too. In principle, you could create a painting that is considered to be beautiful all over the world. And although tastes differ – both culturally and personally – this knowledge of universal, dominant forms is crucial for product developers. Of course, there are still cultural differences in dominant designs. Southern countries often opt for frivolous, playful designs, while those in the north often choose minimalist and mathematical forms – but the basis is the same.

TIMELESS BEAUTY Timeless beauty also exists. Although preferences change over the centuries, some aspects of beauty appreciation remain forever. Visual perception is the sum of different impressions which are closely linked to the collective unconscious. For example, the association of 'if it glows, it's beautiful' has been around for centuries. This is because shining is unconsciously linked to the hardness of a product, which we associate with power and invincibility in battle. So we are socially programmed to appreciate the beauty of the things that previous cultures liked.

LOOKING FOR DOMINANT DESIGNS   The designers at Jaga are constantly trying to find an iconic archetype, a dominant design that is sustainable. They are trying to discover a universal beauty that transcends generations and they are successful. This is because Jaga considers design to be a reflection of the soul. Yet a truly dominant design can only be created if functionality and form come together. These are unique and functional shapes that are inherent in people's minds. For example, the shape of a Porsche, the curves of the Volkswagen Beetle –dominant designs that everyone knows and likes – that should be your ultimate goal as a designer.

Nature is the pinnacle of design and it has a huge variety of designs. The urge for that variation is precisely the driving force behind evolution. Darwin helped us to understand that.

BIOMIMICRY: DESIGN MODELLED ON NATURE   We should follow nature's example in terms of design. Nature never really makes the same product. Each design is different. We have regarded our laws of civilisation as sacred, but we are starting to see that the laws of nature are equally important. Just as nature creates unique creatures, we must create unique products.

Nature has created hundreds of millions of life forms. This has been an inexhaustible source of inspiration for us. The most dominant designs are inspired by natural organic shapes. Jaga developed some radiators through biomimicry. There is Pebbles: a radiator with a grid consisting of irregularly shaped holes with the optical effect of a narrow path full of pebbles. The Iguana Circo is straight out of nature – the shape was inspired by the tail of the iguana, which I saw during my travels to the Caribbean. And, if you look at it from above, you can see the shape of a shining sun in the Iguana Circo.

A NEW DESIGN PHILOSOPHY All too often, design is nothing more than a pre-digested form and no longer creative. I strongly believe that products should be as unique as possible. This also allows you to increase your chances of survival as a company. A kind of Darwinian design philosophy as it were: if it's good, it will last.

Many entrepreneurs have difficulty taking this step. That's because they do not realise that *creative differentiation* can also make you successful. By providing different models, your company actually chooses a survival model because you can assume that one of those models will meet with success on the market, provided of course that you bring design and functionality together.

....

Design should not be communism. We must develop new forms to suit individual people. Design should be made personal again and, thanks to functional design, man should be able to influence his environment once more.

....

AN INSPIRING EXAMPLE:
ALVIN TOFFLER'S 'THIRD WAVE'

....

'Change is not merely necessary to life – it is life.'

....

Alvin Toffler (1928) is an American writer and futurist. In his first works, he focused on the impact of technology on society. Later he concentrated more on changes in society and capitalism.

His most famous book is *The Third Wave*. This 'third wave' refers to the type of society we have been living in since the 1950s: a post-industrial period. The wave that preceded it was the Industrial Revolution, which lasted until the middle of the twentieth century. According to Toffler, mass production, mass distribution, mass consumption, mass leisure and mass entertainment emerged during this period.

In the third wave, society chooses diversity again, and moves away from the masses. The focus on knowledge is back, because 'you can't run society on data and computers alone.' According to Toffler, the time has come for personalised products. For him, *prosumption* is the key to the future.

The Third Wave was published in 1980. Alvin Toffler made an accurate prediction. His foresight makes him one of the best known futurists of modern times.

JAGA IGUANA
CIRCO FREESTANDING

JAGA STAND VSK 2010 - UTRECHT, THE NETHERLANDS
MADE OF RECYCLED FACTORY WOOD

THE JAGA EXHIBITION STANDS

Jaga sees exhibition stands as another opportunity for profound creativity. The construction of a stand always starts with creative chaos, which ultimately leads to harmony and order. By working together and testing out ideas, the design team always manages to create something special.

I never do the same thing twice on a Jaga stand. My biggest fear is repeating myself. We always make our own stands at Jaga and continuously experiment with light, colour and products. The design team creates a great atmosphere and always attracts a lot of attention. An enthusiastic and technically brilliant team works on each

stand – and Jaga has built over a hundred of them. Sometimes the team lives at a venue for a whole week: eating, sleeping, working … everything is done on site.

I try to bring all of the basic values together in each Jaga stand. That's why, for the 2009 International Building Fair in Utrecht, I made a stand out of scrap wood I had gathered in the factory, and which later ended up in my garden. The stand was built in a modular fashion so that it could be used in a different way later on. This really gives rise to the idea of closing material cycles: everything is reusable.

NIEUW

dream a f...

JAGA STAND VSK 2010
MADE OF RECYCLED PRODUCT PARTS

JAGA EXPERIENCE LAB
DIEPENBEEK, BELGIUM

JAGA EXPERIENCE LAB
WWW.JAGAEXPERIENCELAB.COM

t Jaga, all employees, customers and even sup-
liers make a maximum contribution. Radiators
re not just created in the design and engineer-
ng department. Everyone has their say on the
nished products. Jaga aims for great diversity.
Vith this goal in mind, I set up the Jaga Experi-
nce Lab: a scientific test centre and a creative,

open workplace environment where everyone
can design concepts. This is where Jaga conducts
research, such as our unique racing concept to
see how different heating systems react under
the most extreme conditions. Visitors can test the
efficiency of the products themselves.

JAGA IGUANA CIRCO FREESTANDING

UNIQUE DESIGNS AT JAGA

The focus on design only came about at Jaga after the development of the efficient Low H_2O radiator line. In 1990, Jaga received its first design prize – the European Design Award – for *Linea Plus*, the radiator that introduced design to the world of central heating. The next award was for Iguana. One of the first design products in which biomimicry was a central principle, it was a combination of a unique design, inspired by nature, and functionality, thanks to the attention to ecology and sustainability. In 1999, Jaga won the ISH-Design Award and, in 2000, the company received the IF Top Ten Design Award. Three years later, *Knockonwood* and *Strada* also received prizes.

They won the IF Award and, in the same year, Jaga took home the Henri van de Velde Award for the best design company. In 2007 Jaga received the Design Management Europe Award. The trend had been set.

The creation of *Heatwave* meant beauty prevailed once more. Jaga worked with Joris Laarman on this. The goal was to make the best radiator in the world. *Heatwave* is a heating system which looks like a Baroque mural. Consumers are also provided with an optimal central heating product. I believe design should never be an end in itself.

1990
European
DESIGN PRIZE

LINEA PLUS

iF
design award
w i n n e r
2003

STRADA

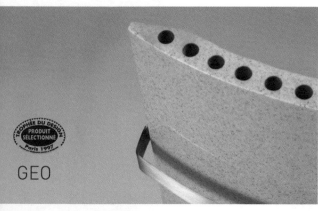

TROPHEE DU DESIGN
PRODUIT
SÉLECTIONNE
Paris 1997

GEO

iF
Top 10
Design
Award
Winner
2000

ViZO
Selectie
Triënnale
voor Vormgeving

ISH 1999
DESIGN PLUS
Sanitär Heizung Klima

IGUANA

HENRY VAN DE VELDE
AWARD 2009
Public

PLAY

reddot design award
winner 2009

TWINE

FREEDOM

SCAPE

KNOCKONWOOD

DESIGN AWARDS

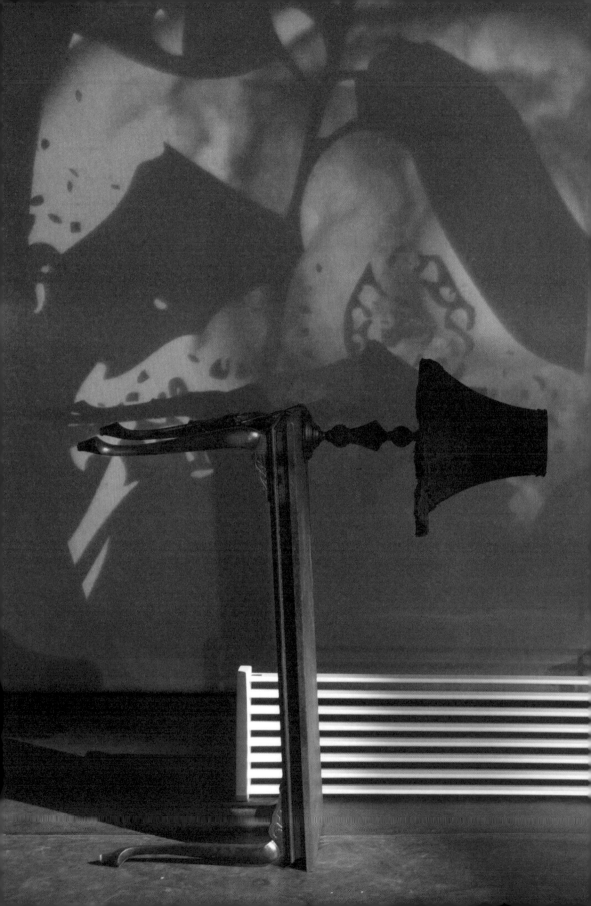

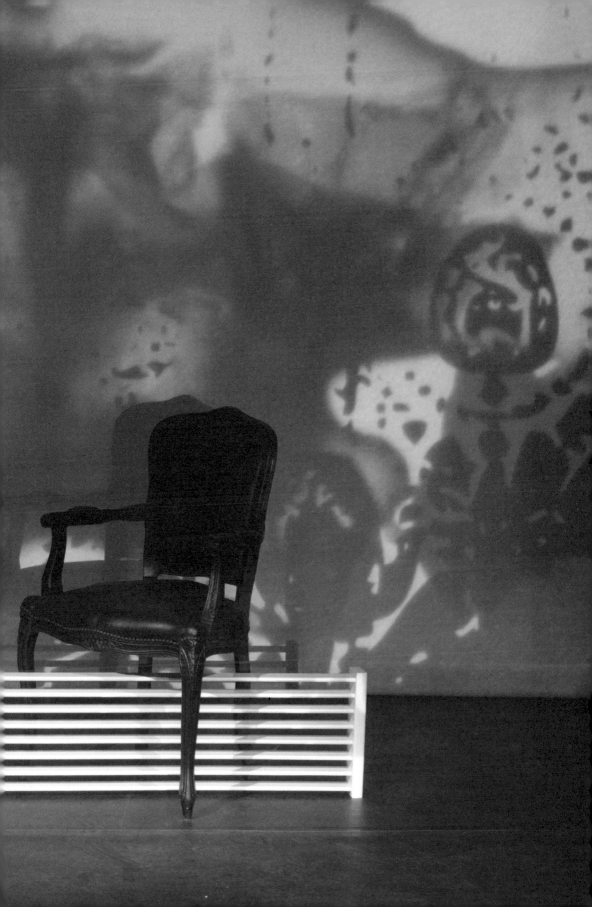

A CREATIVE SOCIETY

The importance of creativity for the earth: sustainability Design plays a crucial role in the search for a balance between sustainability and consumption. Beautiful things are sustainable, timeless shapes by definition, because you can't just throw beautiful things on a rubbish dump. Those who create beauty think about the future. *Respect Nature* and *Awake the Artist* are inextricably linked. Without these two basic values, we cannot make sustainable products and services.

The economy of the future: creative economy The Western economy was in a luxurious position for a long time as it hardly faced any competition. But recently, the new world economies – like China, India and Brazil – have put huge pressure on our economic system *(see page 64)*. If Western Europe and North America want to remain global players, we cannot rely just on our technological developments, existing production methods and extensive expertise. We need to think more in depth. Creativity is key and creating a trend towards a creative economy is an absolute must. That is the only way we can keep making a difference: by combing the best of both worlds – the economic and the creative.

We must dare to think outside of the box.

CREATIVITY IS THE ONLY RESOURCE Globalisation has changed our traditional way of producing. Many companies face fierce competition with emerging countries due to their low-cost products and high productivity. Most companies spend a lot of money on research and development ... but that rarely leads to real production in the West, let alone to export. We must dare to make the step towards new products or process innovation.

Those countries that do not have their own resources will especially need to demonstrate that they have the creativity and innovation necessary to compete. This is because companies are increasingly moving to countries that have their own resources, where they then recruit labour on the ground. If we do not intervene, there will be a total abandonment of countries with high wages, but do not have energy and raw materials available. They will end up in a desert with creativity as their only resource. They can offer added value only by further developing their creativity. Innovation through creative thinking will be the only way to survive.

AWAKE THE ARTIST

THE ARCHETYPE FOR AWAKE THE ARTIST: THE ARTIST

Each of the five basic values has its own archetype: the type of person that every society needs to give shape to that particular value. An awareness of each basic value should be present in each of us.

The Artist can play a crucial role in striving for an open and creative economy, for it is the Artist who helps the engineer to see the importance of design. An engineer's products – however ecological they might be – have little value if aesthetic factors are not taken into account. A truly sustainable product is not only designed and produced according to ecologically efficient principles, but also according to the principles of universal and timeless beauty.

Companies therefore need to build bridges between creative and economic people. Artists take more risks. They are less focused on figures and think in a broader and more flexible way. They are independent of the system and their courage allows true innovation to take place.

By finding a place in their companies for creative people, managers look beyond pure profit. I believe a company should be more like a village, in which each resident has their own value. A crossfertilisation between art and economy … This is the only way we can create a new type of society where it's not just the economists who pull the strings.

Together, the Artist and the Green Engineer design functional, ecological and aesthetically valuable products. But without a creator – a *dreamer* – enriching their ideas, they are rarely able to find revolutionary ways of applying their product. We need futurologists for those products and ideas that lay the right kind of foundation for our future. Visionary thinkers who prioritise one value highly: *Dream a Future*.

VALUE 3

01010101010110101
01010101010 10
0101010 10101010
01   101 101
01010101111 101

DREAM
A FUTURE

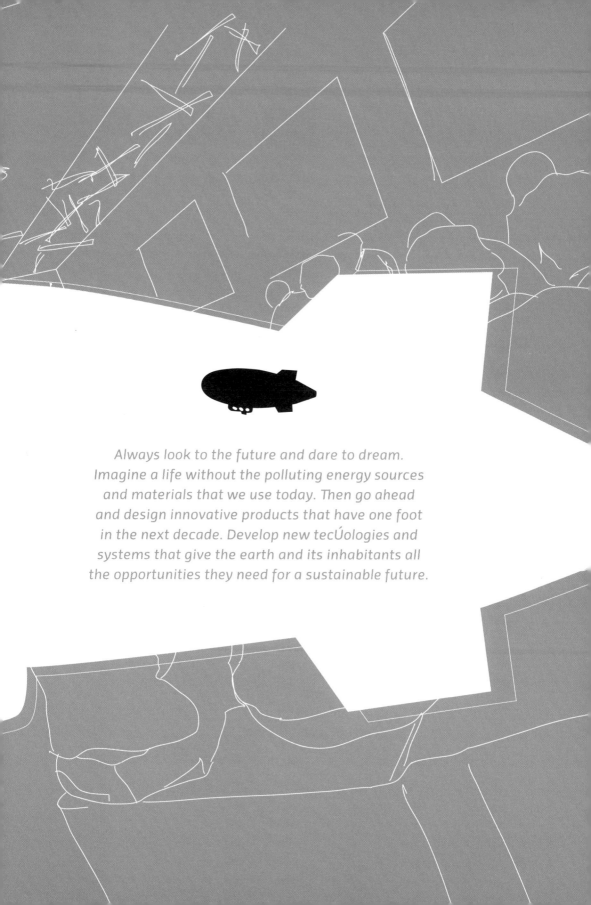

Always look to the future and dare to dream.
Imagine a life without the polluting energy sources
and materials that we use today. Then go ahead
and design innovative products that have one foot
in the next decade. Develop new tecÚologies and
systems that give the earth and its inhabitants all
the opportunities they need for a sustainable future.

THE BEATEN PATH

DREAM A FUTURE

01010101010110101
0101010101010 10
01010101 01010101
01   101 101
0101010101111 101

MAN CLINGS TO WHAT HE KNOWS

Man has a natural tendency to cling to things that have already proven their value. This is, of course, an intelligent decision in one sense because it helps us to control reality and to avoid potential hazards. By experimenting, we create solid principles, which we use as the basis for new developments; these in turn give rise to habits, traditions and cultures. Yet, however intelligent this may be, at some point the situation will change. This is because the world, and our lives, are constantly evolving. Those who hold on to traditions and to the past, stop developing and ultimately get left behind. Slowly but surely, a conservative attitude makes people lethargic and this is ultimately detrimental to our future. Routine is lethal to innovation, because it switches off our subconscious.

Limited dreams We are conservative even when we fantasise about the future, even though we realise that we need to think differently than we did in the fifties. The dreams of those days were admirable: the Americans wanted a society in which no one was hungry and Western Europe wanted a society built on equal opportunities. These dreams have been realised to a great extent. They were based on a visionary idea that democracy should be the foundation of our society.

Dreaming differently It is time to change our dreams because, under the pressure of climate change as well as population growth, democratic society is becoming something of of an illusion. Ideas about equality will not survive if the survival of our species is not guaranteed. Our dreams and simulations of the future should evolve at the same rapid pace as the problems our planet is facing. We should be dealing with future survival models for the human species. But most of us have not caught up yet ...

Letting go of reason and rationality Our dreams are too narrow in many ways. That is because we often fail to let go of reason – yes, even in our dreams. We keep thinking in terms of rational and reasonable logical structures while we should be expressing our basic emotions, creativity and intuition. There are plenty of calculated dreamers, but it is rare to find one who is also a true visionary. Genuine visionaries go beyond reason's constraints.

BANISHING DREAMS AND IMAGINATION

The hegemony of mathematical thinking For several centuries, Western society has rested upon pure mathematical reasoning. We think in terms of a straight line and can rationalise everything in a comprehensive and logical manner. Reason is always central to this, which means that dreaming and imagination often take a backseat. Dreamers don't belong in our down-to-earth, practical society.

A restrictive way of thinking This way of thinking has had enormous repercussions for our economy and technology. By banishing dreams and imagination from our companies, we have restricted ourselves significantly. There has been much less room for creativity because every spontaneous thought has to be headed in the 'right' direction, i.e. in accordance with economic laws. At the same time, our tolerance of dreamers disappeared, because having a creative imagination did not fit into this logic-based framework.

Making a difference We are slowly starting to realise that we will eventually have to face the financial and economic consequences of our conservative mentality. The emergence of new global economies has accelerated that process. China, India and Brazil are threatening to overtake us in technological and quantitative terms, which means we have to make a difference in *creative terms* by building new instruments of survival. And we can only do that by revising our economic model and by giving more room to creative dreamers and innovations.

THE EASE OF CONSUMPTION

By now, it should be clear what I think: our unbridled consumerism suppresses our creativity. By simply buying everything, we ignore what makes us truly happy: creating things ourselves. Yet our reflex to continually consume creates more harm than good. We have slowly but surely lost the knowledge and desire to meet our own basic needs. We buy our energy, homes, food, clothing and pleasure, which of course makes our lives easy, but also empty.

What if? Our dependence on manufacturing, energy suppliers, governments and financial structures has never been as high as it is now. The question that arises is 'what if?' ... What if, at some point in the future, energy were to cost ten times as much as it does today? What if we had to provide our own food because climate change had made it difficult to import food and given rise to scarcity? It is difficult to imagine a future like that in a society where consumption is the solution to every problem. We can't imagine a future like that because those problems seem very far away. And an unfortunate characteristic, which is inherent to modern man, is that he only begins to solve problems when they occur.

Looking for preventive answers I shouldn't need to stress the necessity of solving problems preventatively. An awareness of climate change should have long been something present in the soul and mind of every man. But if that had really happened, then we would obviously already have an answer to those nagging 'what if?' questions.

The key lies with the visionaries, the dreamers among us. They play a crucial role in our future because they see the answer before the question has been posed. They manage to shape the future with sustainable solutions and these consistently lead to a central idea: self-sufficiency. The starting point is innovating with clean technology and the result will be a lower level of entropy, and thus a sustainable future.

"BOOST INTO THE FUTURE" PARTY
LAUNCH OF THE "DYNAMIC BOOST" PRODUCT RANGE

THE
PATH
OF
INNOVATION

DREAM
A FUTURE

0101010 010110101
010101010 10
0101010 0101010
01   101 101
010101010 11 101

MAN CLINGS TO WHAT HE KNOWS
DARE TO DREAM BOLD DREAMS

Visionary imagination Imagining something out of nothing: visionary imagination is man's strength and power. Humans have the capacity to project something into the future and to take all the necessary intermediary steps to achieving that project. This mental tool allows us to fantasise about worlds, forms of society, products and events that don't exist yet. This allows us to transform our reality as necessary. Our imagination allows us to think across time and space. This capacity for imagination is the foundation of our power to survive.

Humans have the imaginative capacity to project something into the future and to take all the necessary steps to actually achieving that.

When I speak of visionary imagination, I am not talking about unconscious, unrealistic dreams, but rather of dreams which combine realistic and surrealist elements; dreams that contribute fully to the survival of the human species. Because it is only if we can apply our unique ability to technology, science and social issues, that we will use it most effectively.

A visionary dream is the foundation of every visionary idea In our down-to-earth society, dreaming has become a matter of courage. Yet every visionary idea started with an image or dream that seemed to be no more than pure fantasy at first glance. Travelling to the moon was one of these visionary ideas based on a dream, and the first manifestation of that dream undoubtedly needed a good dose of courage. Neil Armstrong and Buzz Aldrin landed on the moon with Apollo 11 in 1969, but several visionary steps had preceded that moment, as well as periods of intense doubt about the feasibility of the whole mission.

Visionaries have always needed to have a thick skin because dreaming involves daring, and courage is the foundation of innovation. In the second half of the nineteenth century, Thomas Edison – who made the first light bulb in 1879 – said: 'We will make electric light so cheap that only the rich will burn candles.' His statement was controversial and meant he was ridiculed by scientists and policymakers alike. In retrospect, he was of course decades ahead of his time. That is what often happens to visionary thinkers: people laugh at their ideas – they are 'just dreamers'.

The courage of the Visionary has become crucial to their chances of success. From Tim Berners-Lee, inventor of the worldwide web, to Ray Tomlison, the man who sent the first email in 1971 and Martin Cooper, who conducted the first conversation by mobile phone two years later – they were all called crazy when they first dared to talk about their ideas publicly. Yet the sceptics have been proven wrong ...

BANISHING DREAMS AND IMAGINATION
EMBRACING VISIONARIES

We need to start revaluing the unique capacity of man to dream a way out for himself when he is in trouble.

If we know that true evolution begins with visionary dreams, then we should also be aware that we need to embrace the visionary minds in our society. They must be given a place and be encouraged to use their gift to the best of their abilities.

Looking at reality differently

True Visionaries have the imaginative capacity to skip steps. They have a way of looking at the world, which goes beyond the purely 'realistic'. We need this kind of imagination and foresight. We must start valuing this unique ability of man to dream his way out of trouble. His empathic ability allows him to dream of a solution both through his own spirit and that of others. This means there is a crucial role for visionaries, especially in times when we need to find a universal survival model.

Realism as the foundation

LOOKING FOR AN INNOVATIVE SURVIVAL MODEL The true Visionary gives realistic input. He sees solutions to current problems. A visionary thinker and futurist can look at our contemporary problems and predict what the world will look like within a certain number of years. He accepts that our planet is suffering from pollution, over-population, mass consumption and the depletion of resources. He realises that we are putting too much pressure on our planet to ensure we can live comfortably in the long term. He knows that this situation is unsustainable and that we should deal with our planet in a different way. Because if we do not develop an innovative model, then our world will be even more severely affected by climate change, habitat changes and migration flows and the conflicts arising from these. True Visionaries dream about the future and look for ways to solve the problems we will face in that future. Visionary architects such as Vincent Callebaut and Luc Schuiten *(see box, page 156)* are designing the buildings and cities of tomorrow.

PROSUMPTION AS A VISIONARY IDEA One of the great futurologists and thinkers was addressed in the previous chapter: Alvin Toffler *(see box, page 130).* He indicated concretely thirty years ago that the wave of industrial society was over. That wave would make way for a third wave – that of the knowledge economy. He based his reasoning on the realistic conclusion that knowledge is unlimited, in contrast with the raw materials on which the industrial economy was based. Knowledge and creativity can be transmitted, shared and strengthened and this creates added value. One of his predictions was that the contrast between consumer and producer – which was built on a purely economic, non-intuitive relationship – would disappear. *Prosumption* would become the norm. The fact that his ideas were visionary is now clear. It was realism that formed the foundation for these ideas; it certainly wasn't just an unrealistic dream.

ACHIEVABLE DREAMS The same applies to the inventors discussed earlier. Edison, Berners-Lee, Tomlison, Cooper ... all of them based their ideas on an attainable reality, even though not everyone shared their opinion. Thanks to their realistic input, they showed that their ideas were more than just pure fantasy and thus laid the foundation for even more inventions which progress would bring from others. The path from the idea to its realisation was full of twists and turns, but it was there. And although the final destination might have only been feasible in their own heads, they had the perseverance to prove the doubters and sceptics wrong.

Sinking the old ship: tabula rasa

GOING OFF THE BEATEN TRACK The fact that we have visionary thinkers available to allow us to reach new heights in our evolution, ensures our survival. Technological, scientific and social progress has got us to where we are today. We have tried to overtake time, but now we are being overtaken by nature. We need to develop ecological and sustainable ways to develop

A path is created by walking it. But those who keep walking on the same path don't evolve.

our future, and we can only do that by cleaning up our current ideas. We must imagine a life without the resources that we currently take for granted. In this sense, futurologists are 'what if' thinkers. They ask the necessary and fundamental questions: what if there were to be fewer resources available? What if there were no energy supplies left? What if there were 10 billion people living on earth? Then these thinkers try to answer these questions realistically, even if they have to set pure reason and mathematics aside in order to do so.

STOP WORSHIPPING MATHEMATICAL MINDS It is clear to me why we have been overtaken by nature: Western society has glorified the mathematical mind for far too long. We have thought about time and the availability of raw materials in a linear fashion because we found organic growth to be too slow. Our rational mind has started to regard time as something infinite and that has limited us in our inventiveness. Yet in our subconscious, we feel that unbridled adoration for the rational mind is not based on the right motives – that we have deceived ourselves. Our thinkers must start thinking in a more intuitive way once more. That's the only way they can keep up with nature's speedy evolution and create room for the cooperation that is essential to planning and developing a self-sufficient system. In addition, we need to take the parameters of nature – and not our current society – as a basis. Mother Nature, the pyramid of life, is constantly changing. She is adapting and it's precisely that capability that we need to be able to move forward.

TRADITION AND ROUTINE: COMFORTABLE AND POPULAR SHELTERS In ancient Indian culture, people lived and thought in an organic way. This is still the case in Eastern cultures. Thinkers and visionaries who deviate from the traditional path have a place in society and policymakers appreciate them. Western philosophy, on the other hand, relies on the idea that capital, time efficiency and conservatism should always be central. This means doing more of the same if there is evidence that it has been efficient. But just because something was effective at some point doesn't mean that it will be in the future. If we do not take natural balance into account, then we will eventually lose some efficiency.

This is why we should dare to let go of what we know today. We should no longer hide behind traditions, rules and laws, and there should be no more short-term thinking. *Tabula rasa*: let's wipe away that which is based on wrong reasons, and start again. We should be daredevils, not calculators!

A new vessel: sustainability

VISIONARY IDEAS AS A BASIS FOR SUSTAINABLE PRODUCTS Using visionary ideas to create innovative and sustainable products: therein lies the recipe for a new future. All the new technology we develop should lead to sustainability and the things we make should be long-lasting and clean – otherwise there's no point at all. If we look at the results of our production and consumption along with the pollution it causes, then it is clear that we create nothing but decline. Despite the resistance that is now emerging under the influence of economic and political compulsions, the step towards sustainability is inevitable. Clean technology should be our motive. We need to clean up what we have polluted and the things we produce from now on must be clean and pure. Zero carbon emission is our ultimate goal.

SUSTAINABILITY AS A UNIVERSAL PROJECT The reasoning surrounding a clean future must become universal. The economy is currently the only area in which we think globally, despite the fact that we urgently need to look together for a survival model for the future. This is because global warming is a much bigger problem than just another financial crisis: it is the problem that transcends all others. Because without a planet that sustains life, all of our economic, social and democratic systems will be doomed. This makes universal cooperation urgent and necessary and we cannot ignore this. We need to bring visionary thinkers from all cultures together so that they can form solutions that society can implement.

We need to give visionaries the task of shaping our future, creating survival models for the future by developing new tecÚology that uses up less energy and resources and is environmentally friendly. That should be our ultimate objective. Everything else is a detour ... or even a deterioration.

EXAMPLES OF VISIONARY THINKING

VINCENT CALLEBAUT'S ECO-TOWNS

Vincent Callebaut (1977), a Belgian architect, designs futuristic cities that are self-sufficient and thus looks for solutions to environmental issues and overpopulation.

SELF-REGULATING BIOTOPES Callebaut creates biotopes that regulate themselves and can maximise our ability to survive. Material cycles are central: we lose nothing and waste doesn't exist. Alternative energy sources – solar, wind and biomass – provide electricity and heating to these mini-cities. Production and consumption are united since the residents grow their own food.

READY FOR THE CLIMATE EXODUS Callebaut designed Lilypad, a floating city which prepares the world for the climate exodus. The Ecopolis can provide shelter to fifty thousand climate refugees and is completely self-sufficient. The project thus responds to problems related to climate, biodiversity, water and health. The floating structure consists of three ports and three mountains surrounding an artificial lake which collects and purifies rainwater. The lake is located below sea level and keeps the city in balance. The people work, live and relax in constant harmony with nature. The design is also a beautiful example of biomimicry: the leaf of the water plant Amazonia Victoria Regia was the inspiration for the design. The Ecopolis can be constructed from polyester fibres and a layer of titanium dioxide, which has a purifying function thanks to UV radiation. Lilypad uses only alternative energy sources and does not emit any carbon dioxide: the transition to zero carbon emission has been set in motion.

BUILDING ECO-POSITIVELY In his designs, the visionary architect opts for what he calls 'eco-pos-itive architecture'. Nature and technology go hand in hand in all of his projects. This is why he brings together several archetypes in his company: he doesn't just work with engineers but also with biologists and landscape architects.

LUC SCHUITEN'S VEGETAL CITIES

Belgian architect Luc Schuiten uses the same philosophy to develop his vegetal cities: a cross-fertilisation between architecture, botany, futurology and design. He looks at our current cities from a visionary perspective and rethinks them from an organic and circular perspective. His message is positive: radical innovation gives rise to a beautiful future.

PLANTAGON GREENHOUSE

It's not just architects who are responsible for the visionary ideas of today. In Sweden, visionary thinkers and scientists have designed a unique food system: Plantagon Greenhouse, a vegetal skyscraper. It is a vertical structure which doesn't take up much space and which can easily be inserted into existing infrastructure. Food is grown in a controlled environment, which means very little energy and water is required and pesticides are not necessary.

AGRICULTURE IN THE CITY The visionaries have based their ideas on urban agriculture – growing healthy food in cities. The United Nations estimates that, by 2050, nine billion people will be living on our planet, 70 to 80 per cent of whom will be living in cities. This means that problems with food supply, energy and water are inevitable if we don't find flexible and sustainable development solutions soon. This focus on urban farming is growing, from rooftop gardens, vegetable gar-

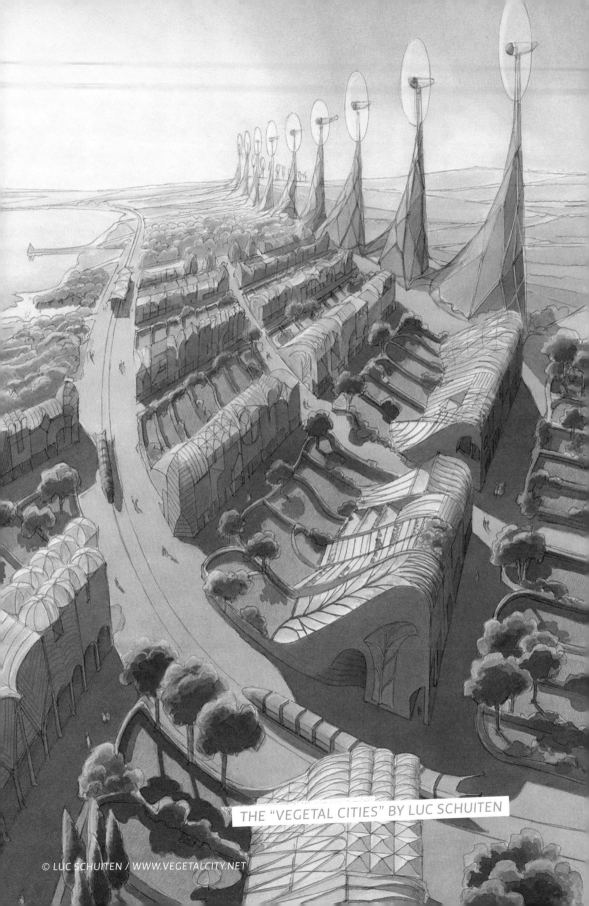

THE "VEGETAL CITIES" BY LUC SCHUITEN

THE "LILYPAD" BY VINCENT CALLEBAUT
A FLOATING ECOPOLIS FOR CLIMATE REFUGEES

dens in the suburbs and self-harvesting projects, to mobile, self-regulating urban farms. The boundary between town and country must, on the one hand, recuperate – so that everyone gets closer to nature again – as well as fade – by producing food nearer to those who will consume it.

MORE FOOD, LESS SPACE Plantagon Greenhouse aims to drastically reduce the uncontrollable flow of supplied raw materials, energy and water to the city. Transport will become almost superfluous since the food goes directly to the consumer, who gets fresh, ecological and cheap products. In short: more food using less space.

THE VENUS PROJECT BY JACQUE FRESCO

Jacque Fresco (1916) is an inventor, futurologist and designer. In 1975, he set up The Venus Project in Florida with Roxanne Meadows. This is an 8.5-hectare research centre in which they develop their visionary ideas into products, books and movies.

AN ECONOMY BASED ON RESOURCES The Venus Project is based on the following observation: poverty is caused by an economy which aims to generate the highest profits possible. According to Fresco, our economy should be resource based. He created an action plan for social change with the goal of achieving a peaceful, sustainable society. His holistic socio-economic system states that all goods and services should be available without monetary methods. The earth has enough resources and rationing them using financial methods is counterproductive. In an efficient economy based on advanced technology, a high standard of living is achievable for everyone.

HIGH-TECH, SUSTAINABLE CITIES Fresco created designs of energy-efficient cities in which technology plays a crucial role. His geometric city systems are completely in harmony with nature and fully computerised, and they fulfil the material and spiritual as well as the intellectual needs of humans.

HOPE: THE INGENUITY OF MAN According to visionary thinkers, the sheer inventiveness of man is the foundation of our future ability to survive. This philosophy is based on a positive foundation: our ingenuity can help us to redesign our culture and thus create a sustainable society.

~~THE BEATEN PATH: CONSUMPTION~~
WALKING THE PATH TO THE FUTURE:
SUSTAINABILITY AND SELF-SUFFICIENCY

The step to a self-sufficient life has already been discussed in the previous chapters, *Respect Nature* and *Awake the Artist*. Ecological thinking and a creative mind are essential if we are to become increasingly self-sufficient. But the Visionary also has a very important role to play in this regard.

Visionary dreams of self-sufficiency

THE VISIONARY IDEAS OF YESTERDAY Visionaries have already achieved a great deal in terms of living more sustainably. They started walking down the path of self-sufficiency several decades ago. The development of technology for alternative energy is one example. Visionaries saw the sun as a potential source of energy and sought ways to capture that energy and put it to use. In the twenty-first century, a large proportion of the population has therefore been given the opportunity to reduce its dependence on polluting fuels and to provide for its own energy needs. In short, we are making good use of the visionary ideas of yesterday and we are building on the prophetic concepts of the past.

THE VISIONARY IDEAS OF TOMORROW In future, we will face even greater challenges in terms of self-sufficiency, because in a world that is increasingly polluted, we may need to start providing our own clean air at some point. Visionary thinkers are working hard to develop ways to provide clean air to large groups of people. Their ideas will be crucial for our survival – I am more convinced of this than ever before. And that is why Jaga is also looking for ways to guarantee air quality in the future. By introducing *Moby*, the modular oxygen bubble *(see box, page 169)*, I have gone beyond our core business because I believe that everyone should contribute to that survival model of the future.

Providing for our basic needs together But you don't need to be a naturally brilliant visionary thinker to be able to respond immediately to the needs of a future based on self-sufficiency. Mastering certain basic skills as a group – building houses, growing our own food, making clothes, repairing appliances – is the best step we can take towards a new survival model. The groups in society that, together, have the necessary basic skills to survive and are no longer dependent on fossil fuels or remote systems, will be stronger in the future. Everyone can get to work now with this in mind.

PLANTAGON VERTICAL GREENHOUSE

© WWW.PLANTAGON.COM

VISIONARY DREAMS AT JAGA

DYNAMIC BOOST EFFECT

Visionary thinkers have always been given a place at Jaga – after all, it is their mental extravagance that has led to innovative and future-oriented products. For example, our energy-efficient Low H_2O radiators with Dynamic Boost Effect arose from a bold dream about the future. These radiators can heat a home nine times faster than average radiators at a water temperature of just 30 degrees. This technology means Jaga has made a move towards equipment which only uses free surrounding heat and makes the living area comfortable using modern heat pumps. This extra powerful technology means DBE radiators are also much more compact than traditional models.

Radiators may also be combined with a natural Oxygen unit which, based on the amount of human activity, provides for constant fresh air. CO_2 levels, humidity and temperature are measured constantly. ECO2FIT software allows the user to monitor all measurements and performance calculations. Along with efficient insulation and ventilation, this allows you to create an ideal habitat. These three innovations – DBE, Oxygen and ECO2FIT – have drastically renewed the heating sector.

This visionary system heralded a new era in heating. Jaga organised the Dynamic Boost Party and allowed this technology to be born in an impressive way, in front of an audience of at least 4,000 people. Specialists from the energy industry witnessed an experiment that demonstrated the awesome power of DBE. Two identical houses were cooled and then reheated. For a moment it looked like an exciting competition. The audience was able to monitor the temperature on a meter. There were two girls in the houses who assessed the perceived temperature. At first, the house with

the classical heating system seemed to be doing equally well. But ultimately, the house with DBE technology reached a pleasant living temperature nine times faster. The heating could switch on and off more easily. In short: a massive saving. The enthusiasm of the specialists who were there spoke volumes – it was the beginning of a new era in heating. Jaga provided its customers, suppliers and industry peers with a journey into the future that day: boost into the future!

HYBRID CLIMATE CONCEPTS

A visionary concept we are still working on today is the development of hybrid climate solutions: multi-purpose facilities which provide cooling, heating, dehumidification and purification. They get their energy for free from the outside air and provide the room with the most efficient level of comfort, day in and day out. They only generate energy when needed and in areas where it is needed. Any excess energy is stored and recycled for later use. These systems are based on ultra-modern wireless communication technology and managed from a distance. The revolutionary principles behind hybrid technology received a lot of attention on the Jaga World Tour and my presentations and lectures generated international interest.

WEARABLE HEATING

Jaga's concept of wearable heating also arose from an ecological dream for the future. Why do we always want to adjust the temperature of the space around us? Our living space, workplace, car … While searching for an answer to that question, I had a visionary idea: let's develop a system in which we can warm ourselves up and cool ourselves down, rather than seeking to adjust the air around us.

GOOSEBUMPS AS INSULATION The first result was *Goosebumps*, a sweater that gives the body just the right temperature by automatically changing the insulating layer. Just like actual goosebumps, the hairs stand upright when it is cold and form an insulating layer of air that keeps the person wearing the sweater warm. If the body temperature rises, then the hairs lie down flat again which causes the insulating layer to disappear.

TARGETED CUDDLY WARMTH With *9 Micron*, Jaga developed equipment that gives off the heat of nine microns, the body heat that is released when you hug someone. The system works using a combination of infrared LED lighting and light-conducting fibres. As a result, energy consumption is very low. The energy needed can be generated very easily, thus allowing the person wearing it to warm up certain parts of his or her body.

ALWAYS HEAT FROM THE SUN *Solar storage* is an outfit that has arisen from the finding that the light and warmth of the sun are lost at times when we don't need them, which is an unnecessary loss of energy! This suit stores up solar energy using solar cells and as soon as the person wearing it gets cold, the heat is transferred to the body.

MOBY: MODULAR OXYGEN BUBBLE

LESS AND LESS HIGH QUALITY BREATHING SPACE *Moby* was developed from the realisation that the air quality in our world is deteriorating rapidly. With *Moby*, I wanted to develop a self-sustaining unit which could take all kinds of ecological shocks and which might prepare people for a different future. I wanted to create a microcosm with its own atmosphere: an enclosed environment that simply shuts out noise, pollution and all the hustle and bustle of daily life. The oxygen and CO_2 levels had to be optimal, and energy consumption kept to a minimum.

DREAMS OF THE FUTURE One of man's greatest abilities is that he can dream up something that solves all his problems. This is the idea behind *Moby*. I wanted to develop something that was creative, sustainable and ecologically friendly as well as providing added value to people's health: an airtight shelter that could keep bacteria out. Jaga had all the technology and expertise available to develop this concept effectively. That's why I decided that *Moby* had to make its own energy using solar panels and had to be capable of heating, cooling, cleaning and dehumidifying itself. The system needed to work with a heat pump and had to be made of sustainable materials and be capable of improving air quality itself. I got this last technique from the active filtering and ventilation systems in the Oxygen radiator.

INSPIRATION FROM THE DISTANT PAST I sought inspiration for the *Moby* concept from the culture of the Incas. They lived in the jungle, but realised that their chances of survival were limited, because they fell prey to wild animals, diseases and bacteria. So they went to live at higher levels: above the tree line, in the pure mountain air. The Incas left a world that was uncontrollable and were thus able to gain a competitive advantage for their kind. They built their temples and developed a rich culture. *Moby* was inspired by their choices and decisions. We realise that air quality has a huge impact on the performance and mood of humans. Optimum air quality transforms man and brings him back to himself. Anyone who spends a few days in the Andes will come back a completely changed person. With this knowledge in mind, we aimed to make *Moby* an instrument that could make its own energy and filter its own air. We wanted to provide the user with a kind of snail shell – the shell that we lost during our evolution and which we will need again in the future.

JAGA BUMP

JAGA MOBY
MODULAR OXYGEN BUBBLE

jaga**Hybrid**Heating

JAGA FREEDOM

FROM IDEA TO REALISATION Making my dream come true was the next step. It took guts to go from the purely experimental to practical implementation. Jaga developed *Moby* as a high-tech cocoon, a 360-degree surround interactive multimedia vehicle that was in touch with the world and the cosmos. It takes reading, sleeping, working, thinking, travelling, socialising, relaxing and playing games to a higher level. Light, temperature, sound, smells … everything can be adjusted. *Moby* creates a special world of experiences, an extension of our senses, thoughts and ideas. An artistic representation of *Moby* is now included in '*Huis van de Toekomst*' ('House of the Future'), an initiative by Living Tomorrow. Temperature control in the 'houses of the future' in Brussels and Amsterdam is being done entirely by way of Jaga technology.

KEEP DREAMING BOLDLY After the initial creation of *Moby*, I could of course have gone much further with my dreams … Wouldn't it be great if everyone could grow a bio bubble like this in their own garden, just as an egg can create a new life form from egg white and a yolk? A *Moby* could develop its own personality and maintain telepathic contact with other bio bubbles and, at the same time, create one brain – or even a part of a brain to share with others. What if everyone had a *Moby* available to them? Then human creativity would become infinite, fantasy would become reality. Anything would be possible in a brain game like this one … We must dare to dream that big. That is how visionary our ideas need to be!

THE ROAD IS OPEN Meanwhile, Jaga has taken steps in terms of technology in order to realise my visionary dreams. The moment of concrete implementation is drawing closer. For example, Jaga has made a significant intermediate step with Grupo Torcello in the Buenos Aires Forum in Argentina. As part of this project by architect Julio Torcello, we are actually producing a huge *Moby*, a completely unique biotope, cut off from the rest of the world. The 1,000-metre tower – shaped like a human genome – is sustainable and cleans itself. Water is generated by allowing the tip to freeze and then thaw. Jaga is developing fully self-sufficient, clean energy and oxygen systems for this futuristic tower.

The uses of Oxygen Bubble technology are endless and interest in this is growing every day. I was asked to build a complete park with Oxygen Bubbles in China so that people can relax in an ideal temperature and in clean air at the weekend.

This principle also got a lot of attention from the Olympic committee. I presented my concept to the organisers of the 2016 Olympic Games in Brazil. They are currently examining the groundbreaking capabilities of innovative air purification systems and they see a double advantage. One of the biggest concerns of the games' organisers is the air quality for the athletes and visitors who will be gathering there from all over the world. An optimal level of oxygen and clean air is crucial. The other advantage of Oxygen technology is that, if we make stadiums into bubbles, we give them a second life, because we can close them in case of bacteriological or climatic threats. This means you immediately create spaces that can serve as a shelter for large groups of people at a later date.

TOWER OF GRUPO TORCELLO

The oXygen radiator

JAGA OXYGEN EXPERIENCE PARTY

THE ARCHETYPE FOR DREAM A FUTURE: THE VISIONARY

As with *Respect Nature* and *Awake the Artist,* this value has its own archetype: the type of person that we need in every form of society to give shape to that particular basic value. Awareness of these key values must be present in each of us.

Nowadays, Visionaries are given little or no place in companies, even though they are the source of true innovation. Companies should stimulate people's imaginations because forward-looking thinkers are essential for new developments. They think further ahead than just tomorrow, thus creating more valuable products, services, emotions and insights. The foundation lies with the Visionary, who devises concepts. The Green Engineer and Artist then go on to implement those ideas.

An open-minded company that reserves a place for visionary thinkers provides several opportunities for innovation. If, as an entrepreneur, you give dreamers the freedom and space to fantasise about and imagine things, then they will go on to do great things. You need this archetype in your business to create groundbreaking products and ideas.

Of course, no company has a place for dreamers who just spout off ideas based on far-fetched fantasies. The basis of their dreams should be realistic. Only then can innovation and planetary profitability go together. That boundary between fantasy and vision is very thin because it is an inherent characteristic of visionary dreams that they appear to be far-fetched and unrealistic at first. An open entrepreneurial spirit is therefore crucial.

Not every company has one Visionary at its disposal who consistently produces lots of innovative ideas. And that's not really necessary because every person has the ability to dream. It's up to each company to awake that spirit and to release the dreams within each employee.

But what happens when the dreams are conceptualised and you have put the Artist and the Green Engineer to work? The ultimate realisation and dissemination of your innovative product, service or idea requires you to turn to the fourth value: *Create Emotion.* Visionary concepts can come to life, and dreams can become reality, only if they have collective support. If we manage to work together, we can overcome all practical objections and realise these concepts on a large scale to create a future global survival model.

VALUE 4

CREATE EMOTION

Share your passion and emotion because unique experiences are a lot weightier than products. Put your heads together as part of the quest to find survival models for the future. Invent, create and experience things together because the greatest gift is never a product, but rather a feeling.

OPEN INNOVATIE

INDIVIDUALISM

In our modern Western society, the individual is given priority. We judge each other based on personal performance and achievements. Self-development and the individual personality are key. The disadvantages associated with this mentality are becoming increasingly clear. People have not only begun to distance themselves from the society of which they form an integral part, but also – however contradictory this may seem – from themselves. They sometimes get lost because they see themselves as being separate from certain elements inherent to nature, elements which have in fact helped them come this far over the course of hundreds of thousands of years. In a world that pays increasingly less attention to nature and retains few group rituals and traditions, people no longer have any reference points. Man has denied the very thing that created him and has begun to see himself as an individual, separate from nature.

By seeing ourselves as individuals, we deny our creator – nature. This means we have lost our way.

FROM INTENSIVE COOPERATION TO AN ISLAND MENTALITY The contrast of this thinking with that of the past is enormous. When man was constantly migrating from one energy source to another, he was much more dependent on the group. During exhausting, week-long trips, the strong protected the weak from potential and real dangers. Food was shared and working together was the foundation of living together. And it's precisely that foundation that is being shaken in modern times. We gradually started to settle in one fixed position and allowed our basic needs to be fulfilled by bringing everything to us, rather than going out to find it. The need to protect each other and to create things together started to lose its importance.

I am convinced that this primal emotion is still present deep down. We just need to find it and use it to tackle today's problems. Those who live on an island and are only concerned with themselves represent a major threat to the survival of our species. It is imperative that we work together purposefully for the preservation of society and of mankind. We need to create another form of collective emotion, so that we can develop alternative solutions to the problems facing our planet today. Technology can help us in this quest – the efficient application of social media means we are taking a step in the right direction.

DISPELLING THE ILLUSION The society we live in now – built on idealistic premises such as tolerance, equal opportunities, the right to an education, pension and healthcare – is an illusion, a bubble. If our economic or financial system collapses or climate chaos and habitat problems make the future of humanity uncertain, then it will be each man for himself. Sustainability is the source of all ethics. As soon as people lose their faith in the system, our ethical principles will disappear. If there is no longer certainty about our future, then the primary needs of man and society will resurface and we will only think about one thing: survival. And mankind cannot cope with this reflex right now. The world needs to make a collective effort rather than take this individualistic mentality, which can be overturned at any moment and turn into a devastating dog-eat-dog environment.

Humans and bats: individuals and group creatures I do not doubt that humans are socio-biologically programmed to engage in solidarity and cooperation, or our species would not have been able to survive this long. If push comes to shove, we help each other out. In that respect, you could compare humans with another mammal, the bat, who knows that the best survival model is sharing. Bats are viviparous animals and not naturally inclined to share with others. As long as nothing disturbing is going on, they are very individualistic. But when problems arise and there is less food available, for example, they share with each other and help each other out. They realise that they will be stronger in future, if they are not alone.

Humans have this same kind of awareness: at a certain point, we realise that our chances of survival are limited if we are alone. The group strengthens us. Humanity is stronger collectively and my conclusion is therefore obvious: it's only by bringing together several archetypes and ways of thinking that humanity can develop a functional, future-oriented and balanced global survival model.

EXCESSIVE GLORIFICATION OF RATIONALITY

Putting rationality on a pedestal It is not just the individual that we have put on a pedestal in our culture, but also rationality and reason. This was already clear in the previous chapter – *Dream a Future* – in which I made the case for daring to dream more. We realise that rational structures are only one of many ways to organise our reality. Surrealism carries more opportunities with it. Thinking beyond those things that can only be explained by pure mathematics opens us up to other perspectives on the future. But in our Western way, we often push emotional and intuitive factors into the background, even though human emotion almost always takes precedence over reason. It is not just coincidence that our heart is our memory – our most intense memories are associated with feelings. The big question is: are we going to focus on our happiness (emotion) or on proving ourselves right (reason)?

....

Our heart is our individual and collective memory. Our most intense memories are associated with feelings.

....

Reason and emotion: a cultural difference Rationality and reason are not priori-
tised at the expense of emotions in every culture. For some groups, collective emotion
has always been a basic value. And I'm not just talking about ancient tribes or primi-
tive people. In Mediterranean cultures, emotions are expressed much more openly. I
noticed this when I first wanted to enter the Spanish market as an entrepreneur. Facts
and statistics were of much less importance than in the Germanic cultures. Showing
emotion and experiencing things together was what ultimately convinced people. In
the East, spirituality, the art of being, is an important part of society. Circular reasoning is still present in every human being. There again, rationality does not dominate
everything. The value of a product isn't just seen in economic terms.

Back to emotion Our emotional and spiritual side could be reflected once more in
Western people if we start working together collectively again. Humans are capable
of great things when they are driven by group emotions. The bridge between emotion
and reason is one of the most important realisations of our time. It might arise from
the tension between the traditional values of the previous generation and the innovative ideas and technology of the next generation.

CLOSED SYSTEM, CLOSED INNOVATION

History has chosen for optimisation, exhaustion and being closed Our current economic and social system is very closed. The reasons for this are fairly easy to
find by looking back into our history. The construction of the first fences during the
agricultural revolution created the principle of ownership. Boundaries were used to
isolate pets and plants from nature and this was the first form of domestication. The
next – bigger – step towards a closed system can be found in the industrial revolution. This was when knowledge was shielded en masse out of self-interest. By keeping
intellectual property to itself, industry was able to grow and the industrial economy
to flourish.

At the end of the nineteenth century, large industrial
enterprises were born and companies became even
more exclusive. They had little venture capital available, their suppliers often performed inadequately
and it was hard to find trained personnel. The solution
was obvious: companies started to do everything in-
house, from research and development to production,
distribution and sales. Each company turned inwards
and anxiously guarded its own expertise.

*Our closed system is based
on economic factors rather
than social concerns.*

An unsustainable system Economic considerations – getting more out of something than nature provides organically – are thus the foundation of our closed way of doing business. There is no concern for society and our economy is no longer able to cope with this system. With the advent of the internet, the development of many technological possibilities and a higher level of education, this was rather quickly called into question. A social concern is slowly starting to creep back into our basic economic principles. This is because a closed system doesn't only limit our financial growth opportunities but also prevents other forms of progress in our society. The need for a change in mentality has become urgent.

Protecting intellectual property ... Patents and copyright are the standard. Every company carefully protects its intellectual property. Exclusivity opens doors and a thick portfolio full of patents makes businesses strategically stronger. The fact that they never implement most of these innovative ideas appears to be of minor importance. Competitors are considered the enemy, despite the fact that they might have the knowledge available to develop one of those innovative products and thus contribute to a better model for society. There are piles and piles of patents gathering dust on the shelves of various companies because they lack either the necessary expertise and core competencies or the necessary funds. I believe that many patents prevent much-needed technological and environmental innovations from taking place. A better system would encourage collaboration and thus allow the innovation to take place, something our planet craves.

... means slowing down innovation Those who shield their knowledge with patents waste a lot of opportunities. This might be a bitter pill for us to swallow, especially in the field of clean technology. Our closed system slows down our ability to act. Our shielding of knowledge slowly but surely creates an institutional war that harms sustainability, as each culture seeks resources for its own population. As far as I'm concerned, this is a harbinger of the war that will rage outside of institutions in the future. If we don't start finding solutions as a collective brain very soon, then humans will ultimately become a threat to ... humanity.

THE PREDOMINANCE OF ECONOMIC INTERESTS

The proceeds of an ecological revolution The big question that economists are currently asking is whether you can make money from cleaning up the world. They have been thinking long and hard about this. We have been creating pollution for several centuries but we have so far spent very little money on eliminating that pollution. We have consistently transferred that problem to the next generation and

As is the case with any revolution, we won't get paid anything for the one that is coming.

now there is an ecological revolution on the way. We can't bury our heads in the sand any more, but many policymakers have not yet realised this, unfortunately. Instead of taking decisive collective action, they focus on the potential financial and economic advantages of the impending climate crisis. This is a terrible mistake! And I am sure that they will regret that attitude in the future when they are held accountable for it. In an era in which we have gathered and shared more knowledge than ever before, thanks to the internet, the excuse that 'they didn't know any better' will not hold water.

This revolution is for free We will ultimately need to realise that we won't be paid anything – in the basic sense of the word – for the revolution that is coming. We will need to create an international solidarity that is not built on financial factors. The profit of this revolution will be a habitable planet – the womb of future generations. We cannot go on without this because the planet is the basis of our existence.

If we want to enter into a global revolution, our individualism must quickly make way for a higher purpose, because we can only realise our dreams on a collective scale. I believe that this enormous challenge is only feasible if we accommodate emotions; if reason and economic interests no longer dominate, but rather intuition prevails. Only then will man be poised to take action with his intellect *and* his heart and spirit.

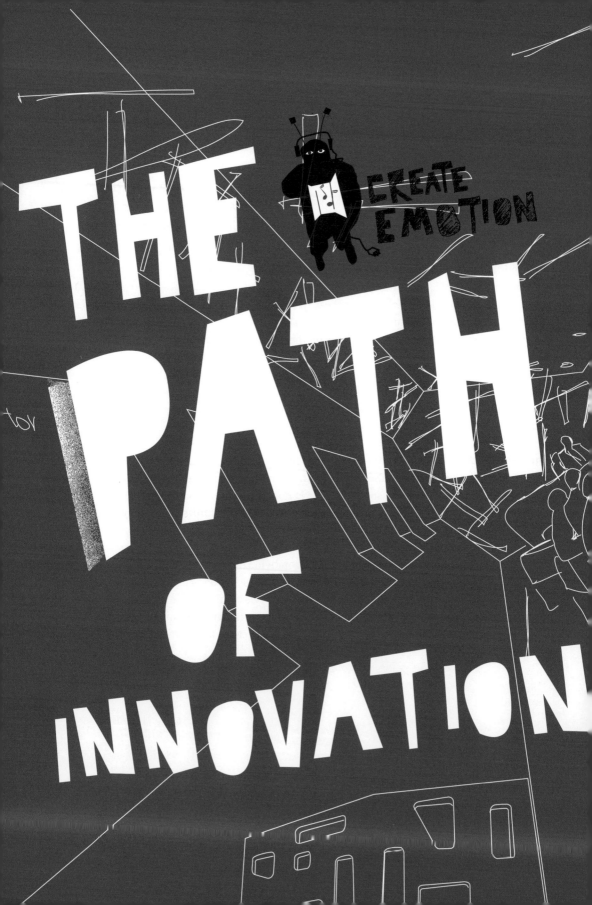

~~INDIVIDUALISM~~
THE STRENGTH OF THE GROUP

By bringing people together again and paying attention to collective emotions and experiences, we are taking a huge step forward. This is because the ideas of the Visionaries, discussed in the previous chapter, *Dream a Future*, can only be achieved if they are borne collectively. I believe that you need the strength of a group in order to realise a visionary ideal. We dream of countering climate and habitat change and creating clean technology and self-sustaining systems for everybody, everywhere in the world. In order to achieve this dream, we need international solidarity.

If we unite the emotional part of our brain with reason, and work together as a group, we will be able to do great things.

You can't impose a dream like this on people, of course – or at least not with the result that I have in mind. Forcing dreams on people is what totalitarian regimes do. Everyone needs to feel the passion, drive, sense of duty and ethics within, in order to build up something constructive for our children and for the world of tomorrow. The people who are able to stir up that passion in a community play an essential role in our society.

A collective dream for real innovations We have achieved a lot in the past as a group, but the time has come for new thinking and new ways to collaborate. As I mentioned earlier, we need to pursue other ideals, real innovations that allow humans to rise above themselves and to find alternative ways of thinking to those of the middle of last century. The dreams of that time were admirable. The Americans wanted a society without hunger, Western Europe wanted a society built on equal opportunities, and those dreams have been realised to a large extent, albeit imperfectly. These societies were built on an idea that found collective support – the idea that democracy should be the foundation of society. Our dreams have to change, however, because that kind of society is an illusion under the pressure of climate change and its consequences. Ideas about equality will not last if the survival of our species is no longer guaranteed.

Linking dreams to emotions works Although our dreams will have to be different now, we can learn a lot from the way in which dreams were implemented before. Those ideals from the 1950s were fulfilled because they were the dreams of a whole nation. The bridge between the idea, the emotion and the realisation was built and the visionary idea was realised by making people enthusiastic about the principles of democracy. If we combine the emotional part of our brain with the rational part, and

If we unite the emotional part of our brain with reason, and work together as a group, we will be able to do great things.

work together as a group, then we will be able to do great things. By sharing passion and emotion, we can achieve so much more.

~~EXCESSIVE GLORIFICATION OF RATIONALITY~~
SCOPE FOR EMOTIONS AND EXPERIENCES

The best things in life are not products, but emotions.

The memories you gather throughout life are always related to emotions. They rarely have anything to do with just a product. You might have precious memories of your first car, a piece of jewellery or a photo. However, you're not thinking of that object, but rather experiencing the feeling associated with it.

There was a certain experience that was decisive in my choosing to join my family's radiator business: my lonely journey through Mongolia. I spent three weeks in temperatures of -20 degrees Celsius, and that was when the true essence of heating dawned on me: quality of life cannot exist without heat. That experience taught me more than years of walking around the factory and seeing how radiators are produced. When I returned to Belgium, I was confident that I wanted to join the business. This was when the idea 'when heat takes shape' was born. The desire to bring warmth to others, which I felt suddenly in icy Mongolia, still comes back to me now – decades later – and forms a part of my investment in our projects.

I believe the fourth value speaks for itself. Those who connect a company's brand to an experience and not just to a purely commercial product are putting the value *Create emotion* into practice. Going further than pure consumption is the overriding message now more than ever.

Prosumption and co-creation rules Producers can add emotion to a product by involving the customer in the development process. Those who are actively involved in the creation of the product they are buying are happier than those who simply buy it. By experiencing the passion associated with product development or co-creation, the unique feeling of a shared realisation emerges.

The win-win of experience branding Experience branding – linking your brand to shared experiences – creates real added value for both customers and the company itself. On the one hand, the brand becomes better known and this results in higher profit margins. On the other hand, you bring people together as a company and engage in sound entrepreneurship.

AN IMAGE SELLS: PEOPLE DRESS THEMSELVES WITH A BRAND The primary advantage of experience branding is therefore on the company's side. Experienced entrepreneurs know that the perception of a brand is closely associated with the image of the company. Customers want to identify with a brand. Image is of course largely linked to packaging, but the substantive, emotional message is becoming important again. A good person wants to buy the truth and associate himself with a good brand. He wants to stand behind the products and services he buys. A company that strives to comply with environmental values, communicates openly and honestly, and meets expectations, will be able to count on solid and lasting client relationships, and that is an undeniable value – in financial terms too.

CUSTOMERS BUY A BUSINESS PHILOSOPHY When customers – Jaga calls them partners – get the feeling that their purchases contribute to a cleaner world, then the benefits for the company and consumer overlap – it's a win-win situation. Companies can integrate the ethical aspect more deeply into their business philosophy without suffering serious financial consequences.

I am convinced that this combination of profitability and ethics can seep through to all walks of life in the long run. I do everything possible at Jaga to allow customers to experience the brand to the full. I want to convey our corporate culture far beyond the factory walls. That culture is synonymous with creativity, innovation, sustainability, adventure, passion, courage, experience, ecology and social responsibility. Jaga is spreading that message at diverse, self-organised events, with our own products. Events include trade fairs which our industry peers attend, as well as sporting events, arts festivals, design fairs, fashion shows and parties. Our employees, customers and partners are an integral part of the experience. This makes Jaga more than just a high-tech radiator brand: it is a community and an experience *(see box, page 198)*.

EXPERIENCE BRANDING AT JAGA

'Jaga doesn't just warm up your house but also your soul.' This isn't just a slogan but also a motto that Jaga has already lived up to at dozens of events by providing experiences connected to science, emotions and products.

JAGA EXPERIENCE LAB The Jaga Experience Lab is Jaga's ultimate realisation of the fourth value: *Create Emotion*. Employees, partners, suppliers and customers work together on new designs and products. Creativity and diversity play a leading role. The lab is both a scientific test centre and an open workplace where everyone can devise new concepts.

In the Jaga Experience Lab – certified by European universities – Jaga analyses the material and energy efficiency of different heating, cooling and ventilation systems: how they react under extreme conditions in terms of fuel efficiency and sustainability. The tests are carried out on the basis of a race system: the temperature in two identical houses, for example, is controlled by two different systems at the same time. By measuring and comparing performances, these climate control systems can be optimised immediately. Openness is another unique feature of the lab: visitors, traders and partners can test the efficiency of products themselves – even online. The lab also has a second test centre, which measures the European heat emission standard for radiators and convectors (EN442)

PRODUCT EXPERIENCE DAYS Jaga regularly organises Product Experience Days, during which everyone can present their ideas on heating, cooling or ventilation. During these events, employees and external collaborators put their innovative proposals for the heating business on the table. Production staff, designers, engineers, artists, philosophers … they all sit at the same table and share their knowledge and ideas. My aim is to include everybody in the Jaga story. During one such week, we created 137 new radiator concepts. Ten of these were developed and are now included in the Jaga catalogue.

In 2007, I invited participants from all over the world to have a unique experience at the Product Experience Days. They were provided with a total multi-sensory immersion experience in various special locations in the local area including a former gelatine factory and a former distillery. Artists, musicians, chefs … all came to share their creativity.

DRINKING WATER PROJECT IN TOGO In 2001, Jaga took its first steps in experience branding. I used the promotion of the revolutionary Low H_2O technology to create awareness: water is the source of all life, but it is becoming increasingly scarce. There are countries that are plagued by drought and that need extra water. A Low H_2O radiator uses very little water – just one litre instead of a whole bucket. I wanted Jaga customers to pass on the water that we saved in a symbolic way.

Together with Vredeseilanden, Jaga built six large wells in small villages in the north of Togo, which were capable of providing drinking water for 400 to 1500 inhabitants. The staff also installed wells with a pump in three dispensaries, giving 7,000 people access to clean water. Thanks to the wells, women and young girls no longer had to walk six kilometres a day to fetch water.

Each purchaser and installer of a Low H_2O element was given a form to apply for a plane ticket to Togo. The winners spent a week seeing with their own eyes what these new wells meant for the indigenous population. The experience was indescribable and meant that Jaga became more than just a radiator brand to them: it became an experience.

**SHARING EXPERIENCES IN THE JAGA EXPERI-
ENCE TOUR** At Jaga, I translated my conviction
about the win-win combination of profitability and
ethical business practices into the Jaga Experience World Tour. Sharing values and emotions
was central to this initiative. I travelled around
the world in a specially-designed Jaga Experience
bus and tried to convince people from more than
twenty-five countries about the validity of my
ideas: from Ljubljana, Barcelona and Bucharest
to St Petersburg and Argentina. By including
customers, employees and suppliers at every step,
Jaga created emotion. The *Respect Nature* story
was still in its infancy and it was during this period
that awareness on climate change was beginning
to grow, along with the realisation that we were
killing the earth. My lectures and presentations
to customers, project developers, engineers and
architects were therefore provocative at times and
yet each event disseminated the Jaga Experience
and made our philosophy famous. Participants as
well as the company reaped the benefits of this
initiative.

**TOTEM AS A CREATIVE SYMBOL OF TOGETHER-
NESS** Another example is the Jaga totem pole
that I had built in front of the factory in Diepenbeek a few years ago. This was born from the idea
that Jaga can connect people in a culture of to-
getherness by achieving something collectively. In
Western civilisation, a village was usually created
by establishing a church. It was a symbol of safety,
which everyone helped to build. The totem had
the same value in other cultures. This idea was the
foundation of the initiative to create a totem pole
for Jaga. Sixty export clients from twenty-seven
countries attended the launch of the new catalogue in Belgium. But I didn't stop at presenting
it: my guests were also given the opportunity to
get creative together. They decorated three sides
of the pole with images of heating, nature and
energy. The feeling that was created by working

together no doubt remained in their memories far
longer than the products from the new catalogue.
Yet this process meant those products were also
given a soul.

DESIGN WEEK IN MILAN, 2007 Jaga christened
Heatwave during an international design fair in
Milan. Patrick Mertens, a chocolate artist from
Hasselt, made one hundred chocolate replicas of
the radiator on-site. This combination of pervasive
creativity, baroque shapes and Belgian chocolate proved to be a huge attraction for all those
attending Design Week. Afterwards, we also gave
our exhibition visitors in Moscow and Toronto the
chance to try out our chocolate *Heatwaves*.

**HOUSE MADE OF INDUSTRIAL WASTE MATERI-
ALS AT WORLD CREATIVITY FORUM IN HASSELT**
In 2011, Jaga built a house made from industrial
waste at the World Creativity Forum in Hasselt,
under the motto 'from garbage to eco design
radiators'. The whole Jaga exhibition stand was
made from aluminium and wood waste from the
factory. Empty Coke cans were transformed into
useful material when Jaga designers made them
into radiators that used energy from a solar panel
which was also made of aluminium cans. The
house, made of wood, contained a work of art by
Geronimo the Jumping Bull, an artist who lives in
the factory and belongs to the Jaga community.
He collected 1,100 Coke cans – drunk by Jaga
employees – and made them into a tribute to the
Rolling Stones' tongue.

JAGA EXPERIENCE LAB - DIEPENBEEK, BELGIUM
OPEN INNOVATION CENTER

JAGA EXPERIENCE LAB - DIEPENBEEK, BELGIUM
RESEARCH AND TESTING LAB

BECOME
A MEMBER OF
WWW.JAGAEXPERIENCELAB.COM

WWW.JAGAEXPERIENCELAB.COM
WWW
THE RADIATOR FACTORY
.COM

JAGA EXPERIENCE TRUCK

BASIC FREESTANDING/104.

A HEATING EQUIPMENT
WITH LED LIGHTING/105.

LOW-H2O TOFSTE

moby

JoBy

JAGA PRODUCT INNOVATION DAYS 2007

LAUNCH HEATWAVE "THE CHOCOLAT EXPERIENCE"
SALONE DEL MOBILE 2007 - MILANO, ITALY

LAUNCH HEATWAVE "THE CHOCOLAT EXPERIENCE"
SALONE DEL MOBILE 2007 - MILANO, ITALY

JAGA HOUSE AT THE 2011 WORLD CREATIVITY FORUM - HASSELT, BELGIUM - MADE OF INDUSTRIAL WASTE

JAGA EXPERIENCE WORLD TOUR SINCE 2008, 35 COUNTRIES, 150 MEETINGS, MEETING 10000 OF INNOVATORS

~~CLOSED SYSTEM, CLOSED INNOVATION~~
OPEN SYSTEM, OPEN INNOVATION

Open innovation means the right to copy and return better. Let's get rid of patents and copyright and a culture of hiding. Share your knowledge instead of concealing it!

Copy and improve Open innovation means sharing and not anxiously guarding the knowledge we have acquired. This implies that we need to get rid of our urge to protect as well as our tendency to shield any kind of innovation with a patent or copyright. Sharing our knowledge can help us to secure our future. The quest for a universal survival model shouldn't be the work of separate groups, but rather the collective effort of the whole society.

Cooperative entrepreneurship I believe strongly that the ideas and methods from one company can help another company on its way. By working together, companies can make each other stronger. Jaga has always opted for an open business culture. I challenge everyone to go off the beaten track and to think about new concepts – for example, during the Jaga Product Experience Days (*see box, page 198*). A company should always free up space for new ideas.

Collective progress Open innovation thus requires a joint effort. This often fails because many companies and institutes are too focused on their own benefits. We will only see long-term results if we are guided by a collective interest. And it is perhaps precisely for that reason that the idea of open innovation still encounters opposition in many companies and organisations; they cannot sacrifice their self-interest even partially in favour of joint progress.

The East as an example In the East, they have understood the principles of open innovation. The way Asian cultures deal with knowledge and organisation has a huge positive impact on technological development. Companies sometimes employ as many as three hundred thousand people, which means their organisational ability is huge. In principle, all knowledge is public property and copyright doesn't exist in practice. The right to copy new technologies and improve the innovation model is thus very fast and dynamic. There are of course limits to the free availability of knowledge in Asia because all countries naturally want intellectual property to remain within their community.

These limitless possibilities of open innovation have effectively been eliminated in the West during the past fifty years, despite the fact that we could yield many benefits from it. Each company's patents impede innovation within their own community. If the emphasis is always on directly measurable financial performance, short-term re-

FROM GARBAGE TO ECO DESIGN RADIATORS
MADE OF EMPTY COCA COLA CANS

TRIBUTE TO "THE ROLLING STONES" TONGUE
BY GERONIMO AKA JUMPING BULL

sults and commercial interests, then real innovation doesn't stand a chance. A drastic change of mentality in companies and in government is crucial for creating positive future prospects.

Crisis as a catalyst for a drive for innovation In an earlier chapter, I highlighted the fact that times of crisis act as a strong catalyst for creativity and enterprise. The oil crises of the 1970s showed that solidarity and a sense of shared destiny can have a major impact on technological progress. There was a great urge to innovate in the development of energy efficient appliances during those difficult years. But once oil prices dropped again, this willingness disappeared and because this was not pursued during the 1980s, ecological innovation almost came to a standstill for several decades. We have turned back the clock. Businesses, consumers and governments need to show the same courage as they did during that period of dizzyingly high oil prices.

The solidarity and shared destiny that arise during a crisis have a major impact on tecÚological innovation.

We are at the beginning of a major climate transformation that will have significant consequences. A scarcity of energy, raw materials and food, which is on the horizon, makes sustainability and clean technology top priorities in the global economy. Companies should start collectively opening their doors to the most diverse groups of people: economists, ecologists, artists, visionaries. By allowing those with different talents to work on a solution together, while simultaneously convincing the global population of a number of key basic values, we increase our chances of success in finding an efficient model for survival. By sharing knowledge and building networks, we can truly be innovative.

~~PREDOMINANCE OF ECONOMIC INTERESTS~~
INDUSTRIAL HUMANISM IN THE WORLD OF BUSINESS

I believe that *industrial humanism* is the future. Motivated employees are inherently more valuable and a company should be a community in which a value-based culture of solidarity prevails. This gives employees the feeling that together they are creating excellent products and emotions and that every little cog in the system is important in achieving an optimal result. They feel that when an idea is thrown their way,

Companies need to find the balance between economic interests and idealist values.

they don't need to ignore it but rather they should have the urge to improve upon that idea before throwing it back. It is like a kind of table tennis game in which everyone is constantly improving.

We can subsequently extend that industrial humanism to the entire eco-economic system. The ideas from one activity can help and strengthen other activities. This allows ethical and balanced business to be a yardstick. Every business needs to find a balance between business principles and idealistic values: cooperative entrepreneurship.

I am convinced of the idea of business as a community. People can excel when they feel good in a company thanks to its specific values and goals. A motivated entrepreneur can make his team better by allowing them to achieve things together that they never thought possible. I put that thought into practice in 2006 by participating in a unique experience with a team from Jaga: Burning Man *(see box, page 246)*. This overwhelming experience and intense group feeling would change the spirit of the company forever. For Jaga, it was the beginning of the fifth value: *Build Bridges*.

THE IMPETUS FOR A UNIVERSAL SURVIVAL MODEL: GREENFORCE

Prometheus stole fire from Olympus and brought it to the people. This fire brought warmth, light and colour, but also pollution. Now Greenforce is bringing that polluting fire back to the gods. We are turning to humanity once again with a green, clean flame: the Greenforce.

I use Greenforce to try to unite all the basic values and to work with all the different archetypes towards the same goal: a sustainable, green survival model. Greenforce is an ecological concept based on open innovation that strives to make every human being able to support himself. Clean technology is central to this: everything needed to generate new energy must be clean. This is why Greenforce bases itself entirely on the four natural elements: fire, water, air and earth.

Greenforce wants to begin with a simulation flight: a virtual exploration of the future; a future in which there are resource shortages, higher energy costs and more climate issues. Greenforce aims to give every person a lens through which to see this future, so that everyone realises that we really don't have a choice.

Creating emotions and building bridges I presented the Greenforce concept at several institutions, including the University of Shanghai. The idea of green, self-sufficient cities has been very well received in the East. Thanks to the innovative and empathetic perspective which forms a part of the Eastern culture, Eastern engineers and scientists are open to this circular way of thinking, which is absolutely necessary to be able to adopt the Greenforce mindset. For it is not only open innovation that forms the foundation of this concept – we must also dare to think further than the mere physical and mathematical.

This is where the fourth value, *Create Emotion*, meets the fifth, *Build Bridges*. We need to both create the emotions necessary to shape our sustainable future, as well as build bridges between our spirits. This is how we make green power a basic part of our philosophy of life. This is the step we need to put truly groundbreaking ideas into practice.

Start from the basics If we want a sustainable future, then we must develop a self-sufficient system. We don't have the time to start from scratch though – it is too late for that. We must work with the resources we already have: our houses, factories and public spaces. We need to optimise them and make them more energy efficient, so that they can still be used in a low-energy future. In Belgium, houses should use 80 per cent less energy than they do now in order to be truly energy effective. This is why Greenforce always starts with the existing house, but applies a new approach: the polluting fire in every house is extinguished while radically opting for alternative energy. We have done this for entire villages or communities, as well as on a house-by-house basis. This is how we make our buildings self-sufficient and sustainable.

Creating more value With Greenforce we want to put sustainable renovation in the hands of homeowners. They should be able to find the weak points in their own homes. Greenforce helps them by way of blower tests and infrared experiments. It introduces them to an approach that makes their home more energy efficient. The most convincing way of doing this is by using a simulation: what happens to the house if you do nothing? Its value will drop significantly because those who are entirely dependent on fossil fuels in the future will have absolutely no control over their energy consumption and energy costs. However, if we master the four elements of nature, then we will be insensitive to price increases.

Houses of the future: using the four elements as a basis Upgrading our current housing system is not a luxury but a necessity. The purpose of Greenforce is to make existing homes completely independent of fossil fuels and thus create a sustainable and comfortable living environment for every person. We can make our homes self-sufficient by embedding the power of the elements into our way of life once more.

AIR The first step in the Greenforce revolution is insulating the building as effectively as possible. We make the house airtight so that energy does not needlessly disappear into the atmosphere. The result is that the demand for heat – and therefore energy –

BRINGING THE FIRE BACK TO THE GODS
XAVIER VAN DER STAPPEN / WWW.UCHRONIANS.ORG

decreases dramatically. Moreover, people are able to have complete control over the air quality in their own homes thanks to automated CO_2-controlled ventilation and filtration equipment. They can use this to create the perfect air, which we normally only breathe on mountaintops: clean air which is free from pollution and bacteria. The idea behind *Moby* – the modular oxygen bubble – is used here too.

FIRE Once the building shell has been insulated and given optimum ventilation, the house is ready for the next step: replacing the polluting flame with a clean one. We do this by using fast, efficient heat pumps, solar roofs and hybrid radiators that can work at very low temperatures and have a rapid response time and minimal consumption. The entire system is controlled wirelessly and can be monitored online.

WATER As Greenforce progresses, we want to make water treatment and water production possible for everyone. Self-purifying water systems will mean that we no longer waste water but rather create a perpetual water cycle. We will manage our water by storing it in times of abundance and then using it during periods of scarcity. Techniques such as making water from fresh air are not far-fetched or unrealistic dreams. Soon we will be using our water over and over again so that we won't have any problems with drinking water, even in times of extreme heat.

EARTH In the future, man himself will be responsible for food production. Greenforce wants to set experts the task of developing automatic, self-sufficient feeding systems such as a food vending machine in a closed habitat beside every home. This type of conservatory with solar water heaters and heat pumps uses air filtering to protect food against harmful substances from outside, and it remains warm at night thanks to clean technology that allows heat to be stored most of the day. The aim is to improve quality and reduce dependence by bringing everything closer to the point of use, and thus decreasing entropy. An industrial organic farm based on clean technology allows us to produce closer to home in a cleaner, more energy-efficient, accountable and sustainable way. The technology for this vision of the future is already being put into practice *(see box, page 225)*.

The final result is a true transformation: a fully self-sustaining, carbon-free society that is in no way dependent on the outside world. The four elements of nature are thus connected by clean technology.

Open innovation: Open Greenforce Greenforce puts sustainable technologies and products on the market and teaches energy consumers to develop their own techniques. Greenforce relies on the knowledge of Open Greenforce for its innovative concepts and services. This is an independent consultancy office and centre for

WORLD'S LARGEST RADIATOR
BY JAGA, POWERED BY GREENFORCE TECHNOLOGY

greenforce

TREEHOUSE IN HECHTEL EKSEL - BELGIUM
POWERED BY GREENFORCE TECHNOLOGY
WWW.GREENFORCEBELGIUM.BE

expertise, which keeps its finger on the pulse in the field of sustainable innovation. Open Greenforce is my example of true open innovation. Several companies work together to provide a complete solution and equally distribute the benefits. We share our knowledge with our clients as well as with partner companies through a network platform in which we allow experts, manufacturers and clients to actively participate by way of blogs, forums and social media. This is where they share their knowledge about green energy and a sustainable economy and create new ideas again and again. They are able to kick back a better ball than the one that was passed to them. They support each other and work together towards a project for a better future. This helps us to lay the path to the fifth value – *Build Bridges*.

The development of a universal survival model We want to use Greenforce to create a new ideology based on the five values, which everyone can participate in. Everyone needs to become a Greenforce value creator and help to spread this new green fire. We are creating a kind of positive green societal transformation that will benefit everyone. Greenforce is our first step towards the development of a future universal survival model. All over the world, people are presenting their sustainable ideas. Uniting them and collectively contributing to their work is the task of the future.

THE ARCHETYPE FOR *CREATE EMOTION:* THE MOTIVATOR

Create Emotion also has its own archetype, the type of person that we need in any society to give shape to that particular basic value. The awareness of each value must of course be present in all of us.

The Motivator creates emotion and thus plays a decisive role, both in society in general and in the world of business. The ecological designs of the Green Engineers, unique designs by the Artists and the dreams of the Visionaries can be as fantastic as you like, but if no one creates the motivation to realise them, they will remain ideas. Motivators get people moving, they set the pace because their emotive enthusiasm inspires groups of people and puts them into action – and that is exactly what our earth needs right now.

Cultures as well as companies would be nowhere without a motivator. Companies need people with social skills and a strong social conscience. These are the people who constantly make cooperation possible because they have the ability to direct others and to bring engineers, artists and futurologists together and then to make a joint project out of several individual quests.

Global collaboration arises from one empathetic brain. By combining the material and spiritual, we build stronger bridges, which allows real innovation to take place. That is our task for the future: *Build Bridges*.

VALUE 5

BUILD
BRIDGES

We should be daredevils, not calculators! Build bridges between materialism and spirituality. Combine economists with creative souls: that's the key to innovation! Bring the different archetypes together to create a universal survival model for the future.

START OF THE "UCHRONIA COMMUNITY"

TRUST, NOT FEAR

We must take the necessary steps to move towards a universal global survival model. But we don't stand a chance without a bridge of trust.

This final value brings together all the basic values – from both the left and right cerebral hemispheres. In order to be able to work on the future together in an environmentally friendly and creative manner, we must reconcile materialism with spiritualism. We must build bridges of trust and respect between the different archetypes in all spheres of society. There is no proven path, which means we can walk the path of innovation together.

Back to the pyramid of life In *A Theory of Human Motivation* (1943), the American psychologist Abraham Maslow presented his hierarchy of needs. The base of this pyramid includes the basic physical needs: eating, sleeping, drinking ... The next level includes the need for safety and security in the form of structures and organisations. Social contact is central to the pyramid while the need for appreciation and recognition comes above that. The very top level is the need for self-actualisation. We want new experiences that make us intellectually richer. According to Maslow, we only try to satisfy our need for self-actualisation when all other basic needs – the three at the base of the pyramid – have been met. And to do that, we need to let go of another part: to grow, we must give up a part of our safe, secure situation. Innovation is always a temporary jump into darkness.

Innovation is a temporary jump into darkness.

History shows that the satisfaction of the fifth need – self-actualisation – is not easily achieved. It was only once we were able to automate work by way of machines operating on energy in agriculture, industry and urban development, that we no longer had to produce food, products and infrastructure by hand and that there was room for the satisfaction of social and spiritual needs. But climate and habitat change has now put our safety and security at risk. We have automated our basic needs but we have done so using the wrong kind of technology. In agriculture and industry, we are now entirely dependent on polluting fossil fuels to provide the energy needed to operate our machinery. If a scarcity of fossil fuels comes about, then a large part of the production of food, tools and buildings will cease. We will only be able to focus on the tip of the pyramid when we can satisfy our physical needs through clean, renewable energy and self-sufficiency. Then our future will be guaranteed and we will be able to uplift ourselves spiritually from individual to collective thinking.

3 x IQ, 2 x EQ and 1 x SQ The five basic values are also included in a pyramid. The base is formed by the first three values, which rely on rational intellect: IQ. Above that lies emotion, or social intelligence: EQ. And at the top is our spirit, or spiritual wealth: SQ. In order to attain spiritual and non-material value – our fifth value – you need to walk through each step, one at a time. You can only be consciously engaged with the higher level once all your needs have been met. Spirituality is really a luxury. There is only room for contemplation if you're not hungry, thirsty or cold and are not afraid. That's when you focus fully on the fifth value: *Build Bridges*.

Believing in infinity You need one basic ingredient to build bridges: trust. Society is threatening to fall apart because we no longer have faith in the future. There is a lot of fear and doubt around despite the fact that the idea of infinity is crucial for the survival of the human species. This was evident from our earlier discussion of the other values. Our ethical awareness and our collaborative nature are inextricably linked to our confidence in a worthwhile future for us and our children.

Free from the impasse, back to our foundations Our society is currently at an *impasse*, or a dead end. We need to reverse to the beginning of the road so that we can follow a new path. We don't have a collective dream any more. The group only becomes of interest when there's a real emergency. This is evident in cases of fire, war, earthquake or flood, when people are forced to create new things together: social systems, laws, institutions, cities ... And they get a lot of satisfaction from this. In other words, people need an even deeper crisis than that of today in order to be able to realy work together. Man's basic consciousness only awakes in the most extreme circumstances. Only if there is no other way, will we return to the foundations of society: cooperation and building sustainable bridges to the future. We can't wait much longer because although many of us have yet to truly realise the magnitude of the climate crisis and habitat change, the crisis has already arrived. And it is now time to take action, because the point of no return is getting closer all the time.

A bridge of trust Every step towards a universal survival model for the future requires a mental bridge of trust. We would be helpless without this. You need to be able to – and dare to – believe in ideals and to be convinced that we can leave the world in a better state than we received it in. That idealism, that intrinsic motivation, is the basis of this last value ... those who are not idealists cannot make progress.

The model that ensures our survival can be found in a creative economy, an economy that is not solely based on materialism and consumption, but also contains creative, emotional and spiritual elements. A change

Those who are not idealists cannot make progress.

BUILD BRIDGES

of mentality is required in several areas in order to reach that level and to build those bridges. This then needs to be followed by a change in our actions; a new culture and change of consciousness which is evident within each basic value, but which is particularly essential to achieving our fifth value.

At Jaga, the step towards spiritual perfection – towards *Build Bridges* – was taken with the creation of the Uchronia Community, where creative souls unite.

UCHRONIA COMMUNITY: THE NAVIGATION NETWORK

'We should be daredevils, not calculators.'

In 2006, I founded the Uchronia Community (*www. uchronians.org*), a worldwide navigation network of creative and innovative minds. I want to use this community to build the bridge between materialism and spiritualism and between reality and idealism.

U-Chronos: non-time I chose the name 'Uchronia' quite deliberately. *U* is a negation – 'not' or 'non' – and *chronos* means 'time'. Uchronia stands for 'non-time'. The Uchronians bring the message from the future, from an era that doesn't exist yet, back to today. Uchronia also refers to a hypothetical period, a kind of alternate history which is hard to define and in which you can change something retrospectively, making the present and future look very different. The Uchronians want to create a timeless zone, far away from our everyday profit-based logic – a kind of reconnaissance within a zone of boundless inspiration and insight, in which creativity and sustainability reign. Those who are creative can do away with all sense of time and feel at one with everything. And, in the end, that is the highest feeling that man can achieve: a sense of timelessness.

A community spirit The Uchronia Community aims to shape the future by choosing to walk the path of innovation, creativity and self-sufficiency. By walking along that path together, we can create a sustainable future in which collaboration is key. We didn't include the term 'community' in our name for nothing: we are fully committed to making the change in attitude from that of individuals to that of a group.

THE BIRTH OF THE UCHRONIA COMMUNITY From the start it was clear that you could transcend yourself using the spirit of a passionate team which includes all archetypes – the Green Engineer, the Artist, the Visionary, the Motivator and the Navigator. The first major achievement for the Uchronians was at the Burning Man event in Nevada (*see box, page 246*), during which our group proved to be capable of more than we could even have dared to predict. Uchronia allowed us to combine all of the archetypes by getting them to work together towards the same goal while also giving them individual artistic freedom. The result was groundbreaking.

GROUP SPIRIT IN COPENHAGEN: THE UCHRONIA ARC The second major meeting of the Uchronians also proved the power of group spirit. We sailed to Nyhavn in Copenhagen during the Climate Change Conference in December 2009 *(see page 70)*. Once we arrived, we docked between the Greenpeace ship and the hotel in which President Barack Obama was staying. On our Uchronia Arc we brought together eyewitnesses of climate change. We collected several archetypes at a kind of 'conference of experiences'. We wanted to build awareness in the minds of all participants by bringing together these very different eyewitnesses around one theme: climate and habitat change.

We also took account of all the basic values in our group of witnesses, from Nikolaj Bock's rational report, to Will Steger's emotional story and Koen Van Mechelen's artistic input.

POLAR CONSERVATION ORGANISATION (PCO) The PCO is committed to a sustainable future for the Polar Regions. Their speaker on the Uchronia Arc, Brendon Grunewald, explained how the organisation aims to make the general public, industry and politicians aware of the importance of the Polar Regions and their impact on the planet. Grunewald spent fourteen months at the South Pole studying the influence of solar flares on the earth and the climate. He was constantly aware of the fact that he would die in those extreme temperatures if the diesel engine in his temporary accommodation were to break down.

WILL STEGER FOUNDATION – WILL STEGER Will Steger is an eyewitness to the catastrophic effects of climate change. He is known for his legendary South and North Pole expeditions. He has covered tens of thousands of miles in the Polar Regions by kayak and dog sled. He has called for the conservation of the poles in his presentations all over the world. The Will Steger Foundation supports educational projects on climate change in schools. Steger has spent a lifetime on Arctic ice and his experiences have made him a true witness of climate change and an inspirational speaker.

EUROPEAN ENVIRONMENTAL AGENCY (EEA) – NIKOLAJ BOCK The EEA is an institution that provides independent information on the environment. Nikolaj Bock is the special advisor on international affairs. He provided a scientific account of the state of play in the environment, which was informative, as well as confrontational.

KOEN VAN MECHELEN Koen Van Mechelen is a Flemish conceptual artist who works with various media: paintings, drawings, photography, video, installations, sculp-

8000 MILES TO NEVADA

ture ... These are different ways for him to express himself on one particular theme: the chicken as a symbol of identity and bio-cultural diversity. Van Mechelen sees the chicken – which was removed by man from its natural habitat centuries ago and is now fully domesticated – as a metaphor for observations on the human condition. His Cosmopolitan Chicken Project links science to art, politics, philosophy and ethics and he was awarded an honorary doctorate by Hasselt University (Belgium).

JAGA – JAN KRIEKELS On the Uchronia Arc, I spoke about Greenforce, *Innovate or Die*, the Uchronia Community, the five basic values and the need to innovate in all spheres of society. Yet, as well as being a speaker, I was also a listener during that week – a student as well as a teacher.

In short, on the Uchronia Arc, all of the archetypes contributed to our open platform, www.uchronians.org. Their stories, experiences and conclusions made an indelible impression on all those present on our arc. We shared information from various scientific perspectives, brought together philosophers, artists and scientists, and enriched each other with our personal impressions. A real example of open innovation!

Creative sharing platform With the Uchronia Community, we developed a reflective and creative platform. The community works as a think tank and navigator in which you and other 'spirituals' give shape to your ideas about the future. In other words, Uchronia provides a sharing platform, an innovation platform that is accessible to anyone who wants to help with the development of a creative and sustainable economy. People have the freedom to be creative in a meaningful way and to look for solutions for a future survival model together. This cross-pollination which should lead to ever more functional creativity.

Getting off the purely rational path The Uchronia Community wants to go beyond the logical systems that we deal with on a daily basis and which are driven by brains that – for the most part – use purely rational software. In our modern society everything revolves around this type of software. Our brains – our computer system – mainly operate on the basis of routine, like a kind of mental automatic machine. Those routines and skills learned out of habit are rooted in fear: if we think that something might be dangerous, then we don't do it.

It is high time that we stepped out of our comfort zone. We are too heavy and are in danger of sinking. We need to jump to a higher platform and we don't know in advance whether it is going to be a stable one. We must make that leap using the technology available to us. The Uchronia Community wants to add creativity, confidence and technology to our entrenched software in order to move away from mere routine

_MESSAGE OUT OF THE FUTURE

UCHRONIA

to a more creative, emotional and spiritual way of thinking and living. We need to develop a stronger sense of empathy which is more suited to our new reality.

Uniting individuals: creative souls unite The Uchronia Community assumes that our society needs more daring people, and fewer of those who rely on calculations and routine. The courage to do this is usually found in those who are outside of the system – we want to bring those people together. This is not a straightforward task because the problem with creative minds is that they often work in isolation and are steadfast in their independence. People who work systematically and focus on numbers and calculations unite more easily in organisations and institutions, and thus give the impression of an energetic and determined group to the outside world. So far, creative people have not succeeded in functioning within these groups and are virtually alone in society. The Uchronia Community wants to encourage creative lone spirits to work together, share their passion and inspire each other and to pass on – as well as receive – knowledge. Open innovation is about being open to new ways of thinking in order to be able to come up with sustainable solutions for the future.

Not just art for art's sake The Uchronia Community does more than simply bring people together through art. It strives to integrate art into our economy by making it productive. We are certainly not looking to do away with rationality and materialism. On the contrary: we want to unite factual knowledge with meaningful creativity and spirituality because you need a creative person to think of something unique and a rational, organised person to act upon this new idea. By renewing our systems of logic and reason and by merging them with more innovative and intuitive ways of thinking, we can achieve a sustainable future. A creative economy unites the mindsets of both creative and economically minded people.

A creative economy based on five passions The Uchronians share five passions: a respect for nature and for clean technology; a desire for the unique and the sustainable; the imagination and desire to create the ideal world; motivation and love for bringing people together; and a determination to improve our world and society in the long term. They seek one goal on the basis of these values: a creative economy, the only economy that can survive in the long term. We aim to redefine entrepreneurship and to increase creativity, emotion, perception and sustainability, because if products and organisations have more meaning attached to them, then our experiences of them deepen and they become less transient. In short, the Uchronia Community provides an impetus for a different kind of economy: one that doesn't just revolve around numbers but which also reconciles itself with values and long-term thinking. This is how we can make the transition towards a balanced, self-sufficient and clean system: the universal survival model of the future.

THE COMPANY AS A COMMUNITY

THE BIRTH OF THE UCHRONIA COMMUNITY AT BURNING MAN

....

'Nothing great in the world has been accomplished without passion.' (Georg Wilhelm Friedrich Hegel)

....

A CITY THAT IS NOT ON THE MAP Once a year, the Black Rock Desert in Nevada, USA undergoes a complete transformation when, at an altitude of approximately 1,200 metres, a temporary city rises out of the desert: Black Rock City. Tens of thousands of 'Burners' participate day and night for a whole week in the Burning Man event, a creative cross-pollination of music, theatre, art and a barter economy. This is where all sensory experiences and mindsets come together. The atmosphere is friendly, open and chaotic and boundless – and therefore groundbreaking – and self-expression is central to the event. Participants build creations that take your breath away in the same way that the sand masses do. At the end of the festival, each artwork goes up in flames. Incineration is an ancient ritual in many cultures. We burn things that we want to say goodbye to – the dead, feelings of sadness, negative thoughts – to make room for the future.

BORN FROM INTENSE EMOTION Burning Man originated in 1986. Larry Harvey, the founder, told me how he set fire to a 2.5-metre tall wooden man – 'The Man' – on Baker Beach in San Francisco. This was his dramatic and creative way of expressing his intense heartbreak. His burning sculpture attracted the attention of intrigued visitors to the beach. Exactly one year later, Harvey carried out the same ritual, this time with a group of friends. Two decades later, some forty thousand creative people bear witness to countless creations and experiences of creativity and technology, not on the beach in San Francisco but in the desolate, sweltering desert plain in Nevada. What was a one-man operation has becone the most intriguing creative/spiritual festival in the world.

THE INCORPORATION OF ALL VALUES The idea of participating in this special event with a group of Jaga employees and friends took seed in 2005. I had the desire to help them discover life again by way of an exceptional creation. The artwork I wanted to build had to give shape to our corporate philosophy and incorporate each of our values. The festival was the perfect platform to spread the Jaga philosophy of the creative economy across the world.

I started preparing for Burning Man long before the actual festival. A year before, I went on a scouting trip to Nevada and, several months later, I put together the members of the community who were to join me at the event during a daredevil training in the Belgian Ardennes. The participants were tested on their fitness, courage, stamina and attitude. Our team members – 43 Uchronians – had to complement each other. Engineers, builders, artists, philosophers … all were indispensable parts of the whole. I brought as many different characters as possible together, even if that led to difficult situations. Yet this is the only way to achieve a truly unique creation: the more differences, the stronger the message.

FUTURE: HOPE OR FEAR We finally left for America, with 150 kilometres of waste wood and 350,000 shoot nails in tow. That year's festival theme was 'Future: hope or fear'. In merciless heat

UCHRONIA

BURNING MAN FESTIVAL 2006
BLACK ROCK DESERT OF NEVADA

and bone-dry air, we built a collective totem: the masterpiece – beams nailed together – was 60 metres long, 30 metres wide and 15 metres high. It symbolised a bridge to a time that doesn't yet exist and became a stage and dance floor. We brought a message from the future that called for more openness, solidarity, respect for differences, creativity, spirituality, sustainability and renewal. The underlying premise was that a creative mind can change the future, but that fear is ubiquitous. For burning is not just one of the hardest things to do, the reason why we were there was always with us: the loss of our basic values puts us all in danger.

THE SPIRIT OF A CREATIVE GROUP The enthusiastic entrepreneurship among all our team members grew along with the group spirit. When we arrived in the desert, there was nothing and we were far away from any structure or regularity. We had to withdraw from all our creature comforts, which was not obvious to everyone. Accepting differences was the first challenge. Once that step had been taken, we were able to continue.

This desert was a wasteland and this wasn't a city on any map. In addition to a work of art that symbolised the creative economy, we also had to build an infrastructure in order to survive, so that we could cater to our basic needs. There was no longer ease of access to nutrition, hygiene and rest and the usual daily reality was nowhere to be found. There was no electricity, mobile phones didn't work, and money was worthless and water far more important. This made working together critical. Subsistence and bartering replaced mindless consumption and luxury. Our conventional model of society didn't work here. These were the first lessons we learned.

A PHENOMENAL WORK OF ART The construction, which had been erected after more than three weeks of toiling in scorching temperatures

of 50° Celsius in Black Rock City, was colossal. It took a lot of perseverance, strength and organisational skills in the constantly dry heat to achieve this. The Burners came from all corners of the world – but in particular San Francisco, Las Vegas, Los Angeles, Seattle and … Diepenbeek, Belgium. Uchronia was the largest and most impressive work of art – as well as the best organised camp – that the organisers and Burners had ever seen at their festival – and it was all done by Flemings. On the internet, the Americans called Uchronia the 'Belgian Waffle'.

For several days, Uchronia served as the most unique dance temple and the freest stage for music and theatre in the world. The light show after sunset was hypnotising. After putting in inhumane amounts of effort in the preceding weeks, we were overwhelmed by Uchronia and yet we realised that the highlight of our wilderness experience was yet to come: we had to give this unique work of art, which took thousands of man hours to develop, back to the world and thus make clear our contradictory message: we were going to burn it as a statement that people must stop burning. A sacrifice for science.

BURNING UCHRONIA Uchronia's fate was clear from the very first beam that we joined together with nails. At the end of the festival, our creation would be set alight to give room to new ideas.

....

Building up only to demolish. Demolishing to make room for creativity. Making room for creativity to be able to start again. Starting again in order to find happiness.

This only works if you let go of what already exists and that symbolism fitted perfectly with our ideas about a creative economy: an economy that is sustainable and in stark contrast to the old economy, which creates too much waste and pollution. Yet all Uchronians agreed that burning is emotionally quite difficult. We lost something beautiful. Burning represents the ability to fully accept that loss; only those who are capable of doing this can really progress in life. We burned material objects, but the emotion will always be with us.

LEAVE NO TRACE A week after the event, it looked like nothing out of the ordinary had taken place there. All traces had been erased – 'leave no trace' was the motto. All that remained was in the soul of those who participated. This is an intangible, immaterial, spiritual connection. In an interview with Larry Harvey, I realised that Uchronia also helped us to contribute something to his own creative philosophy when he told me: 'We have been floating around for some time on what appears to be an open ocean, with only the horizon in sight. But I always knew, or at least trusted, in the fact that new boats and vessels would appear. You are one of them and now, all of a sudden, we have a small fleet.'

NATURE IS BURNING TOO

Consuming energy is paramount to burning nature.

Of course it's not just hope that remains from the theme, 'Future: hope or fear'. Burning the artwork symbolises a painful truth: that so many works of art in nature are being burned by our economy. We create pollution by building our lives at the expense of nature. People are capable of ground-breaking creativity, as well as technological and social innovations, but also of radical destruction. And although the feeling of hope has dominated

since Burning Man, fear for the future is also an essential part of our community.

SO MANY FLAMES IN THE WORLD The Uchronia fire symbolises the amount of energy needed to run a truck for a year. All the energy we consume comes largely from burning nature or its fossils. If we run the engines of cars, tractors, aeroplanes and boats, heat buildings or use electricity, then we transform heat into motion, and what remain are greenhouse gases that lead to habitat change. Uchronia on fire symbolises this burning. All the energy from the earth depends on one big fire. Today's technology accelerates and hides that fire and makes it invisible and ever larger, yet CO_2 pollution is huge and growing every day. That fire is millions of times greater than that of Uchronia on fire. It is similar to a giant flaming volcano. The Uchronians burned Uchronia and as people, we burn the world. We have become pyromaniac apes. Fire has brought us from zero to hero.

TIME FOR NEW PATHS

We create our future together.

For me, Burning Man was conclusive evidence that your dreams can come true. All of the Uchronians came back as different people. Imagining, daring to try and implementing those ideas is now a daily reality for them. They attempt things and dare to take risks because they know that the Jaga community is open to new ideas. By stepping out of their comfort zone and thinking about a new way for the future, they have become different people. The path was created by walking it. This experience has made each individual a better person. Burning Man and the construction of Uchronia have also created a wonderful sense of belonging, which the Jaga community still enjoys today. This is because we are building something freely while still striving to attain the same goal.

UCHRONIA
GATEWAY TO ANOTHER DIMENSION
BUILD BY "THE UCHRONIA COMMUNITY"
WWW.UCHRONIANS.ORG

UCHRONIA, THE BURN

UCHRONIA, LEAVING NO TRACE

THE BIRTH OF THE UCHRONIA COMMUNITY
An end and, at the same time, a beginning … the Uchronia Community was born at Burning Man. This was an experiment in collective creativity and awareness for us and the beginning of a larger project in which everyone could participate. In the months following the event, we wrote a book about our experiences: *Message out of the Future*. We sent copies of the book to innovative minds all over the world, along with the burnt ashes of Uchronia. We made a film (of the same title) about our experiences, which was shown at the Santa Cruz Film Festival in California in 2008 and at Burning Man of 2007. That same year, we screened the film during a reunion of the Uchronians at Jaga in Diepenbeek in front of thousands of visitors: politicians, business leaders, journalists, Jaga employees and customers from some fifty countries. In this way, we invited them to be part of our community. Product Experience Days were arranged to coincide with the film's launch so that each Uchronian and Jaga employee could put the inspiration they had gained during the construction of Uchronia, and living as a group in the desert, to immediate use in the creative process. This gave rise to over one hundred climate solutions. Everyone was pulled into the Burning Man experience. The fifth value – *Build Bridges* – had become reality.

THE FIVE VALUES EXPERIENCED DURING BURNING MAN

RESPECT NATURE

LIVING WITH THE ELEMENTS The Black Rock Desert confronted us with the power of nature. We worked during the day in scorching temperatures of about 50 degrees Celsius. At night, temperatures dropped towards freezing. Whirlwinds and dust storms raged over Uchronia at about 80 to 100 kilometres per hour. The extreme temperatures during the day made us realise once again that clean water and shelter are of the utmost importance. And we also got to see the hypnotic beauty of nature: sunrise and sunset were spectacular, as were the overwhelming, cloudless and endless starry skies.

BIOMIMICRY We got the inspiration for Uchronia, the artwork that we built and the camp we set up, from both nature and deep within ourselves. Uchronia was a strong structure built of small triangular elements, just like an organism. Each beam represented a person who had a strong relationship with their surroundings. Uchronia took the shape of a nest. The wood we used was scrap wood, meaning it was given a second life here.

LEAVE NO TRACE The environmentally friendly motto of Burning Man is 'leave no trace'. The land belongs to the Paiute Indians. They got their desert back in the same condition they gave it to us: without waste or pollution. During the construction of Uchronia, we took care to ensure that there would be no traces of burning. Special mats were laid under the artwork to protect the desert. Nobody threw anything on the ground, not even dirty water. The earth survived the festival undamaged.

BURNING The participants at Burning Man – the Burners – use burning as a symbolic act, a ritual farewell. But the real Burner of the world is our consumption-based economy. Billions of flames burn continuously from oil, gas and coal and are hidden by our technology. Our earth is on fire and we want to make the world aware of that.

AWAKE THE ARTIST

The Uchronians have returned from a time in the future, in which everyone creates products and services for themselves and derives personal satisfaction from doing so.

At Burning Man, creativity and collaboration is a way of life. Creations take place at every level and there is high productivity. Everyone is aware of the fact that creating things yourself is so much more satisfying than consuming.

CREATIVE FREEDOM To a casual passer-by – if such a person exists in the desert – the festival resembles a laboratory of experience for the world's most extravagant artists. Creative freedom is an absolute must, along with respect for others; unbridled freedom with ethical awareness. No one asks questions, no one answers unequivocally, no one passes judgement.

CONTINUOUS TRANSFORMATIONS Uchronia allowed us to build a work of art together that rose above our individual abilities. Uchronia transformed us and each point of view was unique. Three corners, three unique pictures. Each new light cast jagged shadows on the hot sand. Creativity meant constant change. Uchronia filled every Burner with a deep respect for boundless human creativity. Here we rediscovered the essence of working together and realising our dreams together.

DREAM A FUTURE

Everything changes. Nothing ever stays the same – not the sun or the earth or nature, of which we demand so much. We look into the future and choose which path to take.

Uchronia is a totem, a symbol of the infinite creativity and solidarity of all human spirits. Everything is linked. *U* means 'non', *chronos* means 'time'. We are in a no time zone, a timeless place … a place of both hope and fear for the future; a time that links our present and our future.

A PORTAL TO A TIME THAT DOES NOT EXIST: THE 'TIME HOLE' Uchronians are time travellers to and from the future. Uchronia is a time portal in which the past, present and future are interconnected and in which we can move freely. We saw and continue to see Uchronia as a unique vision – the new totem – and return to implement it. The portal to a time that does not exist has been opened and will never close again – it is a kind of time machine. But we will stay here and believe that the future will be improved using the right kind of innovation. Burning Uchronia symbolises the fact that we need to let go of the old – however difficult that might seem – in order to make room for the creation of a new civilisation.

MESSAGE FROM THE FUTURE The continuous confrontation with change and new challenges is a special experience for all of us. But the human mind can travel through time. It can invent the future and is largely free to choose the path it will create – and that path can only be made by actually walking it.

CREATE EMOTION

The construction of Uchronia makes Burning Man the best concrete exercise in collective entrepreneurship. There are no managers, no structures and the organisation grows spontaneously. Everyone sees how necessary their work is and the urge to achieve comes naturally. External motivation is unnecessary. The participants experience this together and are productive together. Together, they create a collective emotion – they don't buy their experiences, but rather make them.

EXCHANGING INSTEAD OF BUYING: THE BARTER ECONOMY

Using this perspective, the festival opts for a barter economy – money is not the universal medium of exchange. Everyone creates a service or product and shares it with others when needed. Burners determine the value of the service or product together. This it is reality, not the economy, which dictates the value of products and services. This sharing policy indicates the true sense of the value of food and water and, because everyone works together on something collective, bartering and being creatively economical happen automatically. And although the term 'economy' is never discussed, there is definitely an awareness of an economy because 50,000 people are living together in a hot, windy desert, far away from the rest of the world.

COLLECTIVELY FREE AND CREATIVE

The open culture of freedom that prevails at Burning Man results in anything but a lack of norms. A large group of people show that humanity is able to live together freely and to build something. Nobody passes judgement, be it good or bad, beautiful or ugly. These are concepts that the participants in the festival almost never use – the only criterion is creativity.

SPIRITUAL PROFIT

All participants are volunteers, they contribute freely to Uchronia without personal benefit other than spiritual.

All participants that I brought to Nevada were volunteers. They contributed to Uchronia without the promise of profit in the literal sense of the word. Spiritual profit was their only motivation

BUILDING A TOTEM

The structure of Uchronia –thousands of boards nailed together – symbolised interconnectedness. Everything was linked within a creative economy. After weeks of intense collaboration, a unique sense of belonging was created among the Uchronians. Uchronia served as a kind of totem. Together we were able to make something that we are proud of collectively – something that comes from deep within us. That feeling is not confined to those who built Uchronia themselves. I invited ten journalists out to Black Rock Desert to come and see our achievement. They were immediately caught up in it and were no longer objective observers or visitors, but rather became participants in an impressive creative experience. And because they shared in the experience, production and emotion of it all, they were able to write great articles on Uchronia.

BUILD BRIDGES

A spiritual experience without precedent. Timelessness and connectedness. The bridge between past and future. The bridge between the material and the spiritual. The bridge to a sustainable, creative world: Uchronia.

We discovered that the best moments in life are timeless feelings. Those who have no sense of time, discover real happiness and the feeling that everything is connected – everything is one being.

TIME FOR A DIFFERENT KIND OF AWARENESS

A truly creative economy sees sustainability, clean technology, reusability, long-term visionary thinking and emotion as crucial components. The transition from our current, deteriorating system of production, consumption and the market to a creative economy requires a profound and disruptive change in our thinking and our way of life. Since the fire was stolen from Mount Olympus, Pandora and her box of sins are everywhere. We must first say goodbye to what we have and to what we are by burning – that's the only way we can really move forward.

Away from pure Cartesian thinking In order to build bridges, we need to go deep down into our original brain. We must realise that a mathematical, Cartesian mind that thinks in terms of profit (and which we regard as the norm in modern times) is not the only approach. If we look only for unquestionable security, then we are not true to our human spirit. By separating emotion and reason so dramatically, we are becoming alienated from ourselves. Our primal brain is based on many more facets and by suppressing these into the background, we have impoverished our brain.

Our brain is addicted. Our primal brain is so much more than pure rational thinking.

Today a single way of thinking dominates. It is economic and rational and over-structured. The modern person must be liberated from this rigid way of thinking and get away from pure worldly reason and short-term profit. No more thinking in a line but rather in a circle by which everything is connected. That does not mean that we should forget the mathematical entirely – but it does mean that we can only create a survival model by accepting other ways of thinking. Creative minds should be able to have more influence on the economy and industry. This change in mentality is the only way to make a change in our society.

I do not have the urge to dematerialise everything, but I do want to steer our thinking and the decision processes associated with it more in the spiritual, timeless and sustainable direction. What is the meaning of everything? To pass on life in a better world. That is added value. I place the creative economy between today's economy and the spiritualism of the East. Let's get rid of all the evils of our present system and add things that we intuitively find better for our future.

MESSAGE FROM THE FUTURE: STOP BURNING!

Those who open their minds to the future are full of conviction for an environmentally friendly creative economy.

Thinking beyond today To build a bridge to the creative economy, you need realise that your mind makes time travel possible. If you want, you can jump back to any point in your past – and we often do. Losing ourselves in memories and nostalgia is part of man's nature, but travelling with your mind to the *future* is in fact much easier because the possibilities are endless. You have no limitations, because you are travelling to a time that does not exist, at a speed faster than light.

This ability to build a bridge to the future is unique to humans. Every being in this little universe is faced with changes and new challenges, but, in my opinion, only intelligent humans have the ability to travel through time. Those humans can see into the future and choose their own path, because the time which is still to come exists in our minds. And in our hearts, we know what we want our future to look like.

Those who think beyond tomorrow and have already worked out their path to the future, automatically focus more on nature. Our exploitative attitude towards the natural elements has led to our current predicament. We are on a side road. If we bring man back into balance with the sun (fire), air, earth and water, then he will eventually learn to cope with his sustainable habitat: the planet or the life within him. This is when he will learn to adapt and conform.

If we succeed in opening our minds to the future, then we will definitely be choosing an ecologically driven creative economy – the only economy with real added value. This is when we will together seek solutions to the problems of today *and* tomorrow. This is when we will find new technology to continue to provide for all of humanity's basic needs without destroying all life in the process.

From individuals to a group
THE ESSENTIAL ROLE OF THE NAVIGATOR: THE SPIRIT IS THE DIRECTION AND THE ENGINE It is a thousand-year-old phenomenon: a group of people travels from one energy source to another once they have exhausted their temporary habitat with their consumption. One person travels up ahead and explores. He seeks a new, promising source of energy and once he has found it, the group follows. This explorer places the group above his own safety. As a navigator, he builds a bridge to the future.

'It's better to do something, however small or little, than to do nothing.' (Ghandi)

We lost that navigator in recent centuries. The seemingly inexhaustible supply of fossil fuels and raw materials and the use of machines have lulled our ancient consciousness to sleep. The economists took over and exploring no longer seemed necessary – this is exactly why we've fallen behind.

Yet the Navigator perfectly complements the economist, who quickly succeeds in tapping into the energy from the new source. We need to send our navigators – along with our Visionaries – back to search for alternative sources of energy and raw materials: the new survival area. It is up to the engineers and economists to make those accessible to everyone and it is up to the motivators to convince each individual that we need a more sustainable way of life.

THE GROUP OVER THE INDIVIDUAL: FOR THE SAKE OF HONOUR The main change in mentality is coming to the realisation that we must place the needs of the group above those of the individual and put society above ourselves. We can only find a universal survival model as a group. By committing ourselves to others we share ideas and work together on a collective plan. By doing something small for the same big project, we reach our goal as a community.

Cooperation or co-creation requires a drastic 'click' in the human spirit, especially as we won't get paid anything in economic terms for the revolution that is coming. Our Navigators strive for something more sound – to preserve our species and the balance between all life forms on this unique planet. That shouldn't be too hard. Fast forward in time and try to explain to the next generation why you did nothing to improve the situation, why you didn't consider the long-term consequences of your actions. You will realise quickly that we can't build this bridge on the basis of old considerations about profit or 'payback time', but rather for the sake of honour and respect for all life forms that have brought us here and especially for those still to come.

THE COMPANY IN A CREATIVE ECONOMY

Entrepreneurs with an open mind To create a different economy, entrepreneurs must realise that they as a group are the initiators – they are the Navigators. They need to be innovative and create in their entrepreneurship. The basic requirement for this is a free spirit. We need courage to return to our economy: the perspective of a child with dreams about the future; a fearless attitude. Entrepreneurs must show courage and renew themselves.

Shifting boundaries means daring to try Real, innovative entrepreneurs tread untrodden paths – sometimes getting quite close to a precipice – as they look for new solutions. Innovation does not need to be a leap into complete darkness, but you can't renew yourself without taking risks. Each company also needs to develop the technology to be able to tread those unexplored paths, instead of repeatedly choosing the easiest path out of habit. That choice will pay off in the long term. You will always be chased by your competitors on the main road, but on new paths . And if you do meet someone along the way then you simply work with them, without restrictive systems and as an open innovator.

Beyond open innovation In *Create Emotion*, I emphasised the importance of open innovation. Companies that want to share their knowledge will reap the fruits of that in the long term. Working together makes them stronger and if they want to go one step further then they can start to *Build Bridges* in which they will be involved in something higher: a super-innovation. They will be involved in a project that goes beyond mere production, sale and consumption. They will use their knowledge and creativity to work on that universal survival model for the future that we should currently be looking for en masse. By participating in a platform such as the Uchronia Community – *www.uchronians.org* – we can take the first step.

THE GOAL: ONE EMPATHETIC SUPER-BRAIN

Invincible Creative minds which join together in communities; entrepreneurs who work together in an open and innovative economy ... This should all lead to one goal: an empathetic super-brain that creates a universal survival model. That is what our future needs. The strength to achieve great things comes from the spirit of a community. If you fight on the basis of a collective ideology, then you're unbeatable and you have the fire to create the ultimate solution.

Predicting the dreams of mankind The Uchronia Community strives to bring all visionary thinkers into one experience lab to try and 'pre-think' the dreams of mankind. We unite those spirits in a kind of super-brain and every day we get one step closer. Our technology, which is becoming ever faster and more effective, will help us achieve that. For instance, social media already provides a lot of additional opportunities and can help to establish the bridge to a creative collective. We have the resources available. We just need to realise the dream of bringing all those brains together in a kind of telepathic whole (*see* Moby, *page 169*). As long as we continue to walk down that road together, acting on our five basic values, we are on the right track ...

THE ARCHETYPE FOR *BUILD BRIDGES:*
THE NAVIGATOR

A true Navigator is spiritual and gets the greatest satisfaction from a moment of timelessness. He gets his strength from a connection to everything and wants to show others the way.

He has a deep trust and his belief in a better future is greater than his fear of what might happen. This is why he is actively looking for ways to shape the future in a sustainable way – not just for himself but for all of mankind. His motivation goes beyond self-interest.

The Navigator incorporates rational, emotional and spiritual elements into his way of life and thinking. He believes in more than what he simply observes. He is open to new ideas and creative approaches and is also able to let go of pure rational thinking if necessary.

Every man has a rudimentary navigation system within himself. But the Navigator wants to share his knowledge and contribute to a higher purpose. He plays an important role in the future of our planet because he does not impose any restrictions on himself. He dares to tread unexplored paths and to take people along with him. The Navigator inspires, motivates and brings people together and ensures that everything is reconnected.

THE KEY TO INNOVATION

The world is burning in all sorts of ways – both literally and figuratively. It is burning in environmental, economic and social terms and it is burning our belief systems and institutions. And that fire is set to get worse. This is why we need sustainable and clean technology while striving to create a society which lives in harmony with nature: the green force. This is when a new type of person – the Uchronian – will be resurrected, like a phoenix from the ashes.

The five values that I have presented in this book are complementary, as they hark back to the essence of man. If these basic values were to be reactivated within each of us, then together we could strive to create a universal survival model. And I am convinced that we can achieve this ideal. *Time will change us.*

To be able to innovate in a sustainable way, all facets of society must be aware of these five values, and the same must be true all over the world. Each policymaker should be guided by these values when making decisions. The ideal organisation includes a collection of these five archetypes – different personalities who think differently. We need fearless and conservative individuals working together as one and thus achieving far better results than if they were to act alone; those who dream and those who rely on figures working together, with everyone inspiring and complementing each other. A collaboration of archetypes ensures that a company does not retreat into itself and stop evolving.

The same applies to our society. A balanced society is one in which all archetypes are given a place. We must start thinking differently. A future-oriented philosophy must allow scope for uniqueness. Inspiration and innovation require a respect for diversity, and only technology and fascinating variety can allow us to work together as one brain (*Moby*). That is the key to a universal survival model for the future. The choice is ours:

Innovate or die.
What are we waiting for?!

WE SHOULD BE DAREDEVILS

GLOSSARY

ANTHROPOGENIC   Brought about by humans.

ARCHETYPE   An original type. In this book, Jan Kriekels links each of his five basic values to a particular archetype. In doing so, he refers to a type of person that gives shape to and propagates this basic value. The five archetypes are the Green Engineer, the Artist, the Visionary, the Motivator and the Navigator.

ASEAN   Association of South-East Asian Nations. A collaboration agreement between Burma, Brunei, Cambodia, Philippines, Indonesia, Laos, Malaysia, Singapore, Thailand and Vietnam.

ATMOSPHERE   The atmosphere is the air surrounding the earth. The atmosphere, which consists of a mixture of different gases, filters the sunlight and protects the earth from harmful radiation.

BIO-CAPACITY   The earth's ability to regenerate or restore its natural resources (forests, rivers, fishing areas). An important term for calculating the ecological footprint.

BIODIVERSITY   Term indicating the degree of diversity of life forms within an ecosystem, including our planet. Biodiversity is a good indicator for the health of an ecosystem: the more variety within a system, the more it resists change. Biodiversity is closely linked to the climate.

BIOFUELS   Fuel in a solid, liquid or gaseous state made from biomass. Biofuels are renewable and are therefore seen as a sustainable alternative to fossil fuels.

BIOMIMICRY   Copying natural elements.

BLACK ROCK CITY   Temporary town in the Nevada desert, which gets reconstructed once a year for the Burning Man event.

BOCK, NIKOLAJ   Advisor to the European Environment Agency. One of the speakers on the Uchronia Arc during the climate conference in Copenhagen.

BURNERS   Participants in Burning Man.

BURNING MAN   Arts festival held once a year in a temporary town – Black Rock City – in the Nevada desert.

CALLEBAUT, VINCENT
Belgian architect who designs fully self-sufficient futuristic cities.

CARBON DIOXIDE
Carbon dioxide (CO_2) is a colourless and odourless gas produced by the complete combustion of carbon. It occurs naturally in the atmosphere. Carbon dioxide is a greenhouse gas which is occurring in ever greater quantities in the atmosphere and thus contributes to global warming.

CFCS
Abbreviation of chlorofluorocarbon. A chemical compound of chlorine, fluorine, carbon and hydrogen that is depleting the earth's ozone layer.

CLAESEN, DIRK
Sculptor and taxidermist from the Hasselt company Zephyr, whose work strives to create a fusion between science and aesthetics. He created a work of art for Jaga in the form of a dead whale.

CLEAN TECHNOLOGY
Sustainable technology that does not emit carbon dioxide and other pollutants.

CLIMATE REFUGEE
Someone who is forced to flee from his or her living environment in order to find a new home due to the effects of climate change.

CONVECTOR
Heating appliance with device for air circulation.

COPYRIGHT
The exclusive right to reproduce, publish and sell an artistic piece of work.

DARWIN, CHARLES
English scientist, biologist and theologian (1809 – 1882) who argued that natural selection drives the evolution of species. Only the strongest species will survive.

DECENTRALISATION
Distribution of tasks and responsibilities among smaller entities instead of implementation by a central body.

DYNAMIC BOOST EFFECT
Revolutionary heating technology from Jaga in which boosters greatly increase thermal efficiency. An effective and energy-efficient system. A room is heated up to nine times faster than when using traditional heating methods.

EASTER ISLAND
Polynesian island in the Pacific Ocean which once had a unique ecosystem and a rich culture. The island became

impoverished due to deforestation, overpopulation and the depletion of natural resources.

ECOLOGICAL FOOTPRINT

Number that indicates how much biologically productive land and water area a person uses to maintain his or her level of consumption and to process his or her waste production. An ecological footprint is expressed in global hectares.

ECOSYSTEM

The number of plants and animals in a given territory and their interaction with their environment.

EL NIÑO

Phenomenon in which sea water is warming up along the equator in the eastern Pacific. On average, El Niño affects the weather in many parts of the world every three to seven years.

ENTROPY

Entropy is an important concept in thermodynamics. In this book, Jan Kriekels uses the term to describe the loss of value that occurs when producing an item requires more energy than the final product produces. For example, a steak which produces 400 kcal required far more energy before it landed on our plates: food for the cow, transport, processing, distribution, etc. Extropy is used in this book to mean the opposite of entropy.

EXPERIENCE BRANDING

A marketing strategy in which a brand is linked to experiences or adventures in order to become more strongly anchored in the head of (potential) customers.

EXPORT LION (THE)

Export award given every year in Flanders to recognise the importance of exports for the Flemish economy. An initiative by Flanders Investment & Trade.

EXTROPY

Extropy is used in this book to mean the opposite of entropy. This means not causing a loss in value when producing and/or consuming.

FLORIDA, RICHARD

American sociologist who has written several books about the creative economy.

FOREST STEWARDSHIP COUNCIL

International non-profit organisation founded in 1993 which aims to create responsible forest management worldwide.

FOSSIL FUELS

Fossil fuels are hydrocarbon compounds. They were created from the remains of plant and animal life which lived in the distant geological past of the earth. Examples of fossil fuels are oil, gas, lignite and coal. Humans mine fossil fuels and use them as energy. The combustion of fossil fuels releases carbon dioxide.

FRESCO, JACQUES

Inventor, futurologist and designer who established The Venus Project in Florida along with Roxanne Meadows. This is where he gives shape to his visionary ideas about an economy based on raw materials rather than profit.

GEOTHERMAL ENERGY

Energy from geothermal heat that is created by a temperature difference between the earth's surface and the heat reservoirs deep inside the earth.

GERONIMO THE JUMPING BULL Artist who lives at Jaga.

GLACIERS

Ice masses formed on land, heavy enough to flow slowly downhill. Glaciers cover about 15 million km| of the earth's surface. They contain about 87 per cent of the earth's freshwater.

GREENFORCE

An open innovation ecological concept which aims to make every human self-sufficient by way of clean technology.

GREENHOUSE EFFECT

The effect caused by the presence of greenhouse gases in the atmosphere. Sunbeams give warmth to the earth. The earth reflects some of that heat back into the atmosphere as infrared radiation. Greenhouse gases absorb that radiation and thus ensure that less solar radiation gets absorbed. Without this effect, the earth's temperature would be over 30 degrees Celsius lower. The term is derived from a greenhouse or conservatory where the temperature increases because the heat remains under the roof.

GREENHOUSE GASES

Gases in the atmosphere that absorb and reflect infrared radiation back to the earth's surface. The main greenhouse gases are carbon dioxide, methane, black carbon, halogenated alkanes, nitrogen oxide, carbon monoxide and volatile organic hydrocarbons. They raise the temperature on the planet, because they work like a filter between the earth and the warmth of the sun. The thicker the atmosphere, the more heat is retained.

GRUNEWALD, BRENDON Founder of the Polar Conservation Organisation who came to speak on the Uchronia Arc in 2008 about the importance of the earth's Polar Regions.

GRUPO TORCELLO Initiative by Argentine architect Julio Torcello, who is going to build a self-sustaining tower at the Buenos Aires Forum. The tower, inspired by the spiral shape of DNA, would be the tallest tower in the world at one kilometre high. It will accommodate 120,000 people. Jaga is involved in this prestigious project.

GULF STREAM Warm ocean currents in the North Atlantic Ocean.

HABITAT Place where an animal or plant is fully integrated into its surroundings.

HARVEY, LARRY Co-organiser of the Burning Man event in Nevada. In 1986, Harvey burned a wooden man on the beach in order to help him get over a lost love. That act would become an annual arts festival in Black Rock City.

HIERARCHY OF NEEDS A concept from Abraham Maslow, which arranges the needs of humans into a pyramid structure with the physical needs at the bottom and the need for self-actualisation at the top.

HOT SPOT Volcanically active area below the earth's surface with a very high temperature.

HUIS VAN DE TOEKOMST (HOUSE OF THE FUTURE) Project in Vilvoorde implemented with the support of the Flemish government in which the technical equipment in a house is created based on the principle of sustainability. This means there is more focus on the use of sustainable or renewable energy and reducing the use of heat, water and electricity.

ICE AGE An ice age is a period during which the earth's climate is much colder than it is today. These cold temperatures have profound geological and biological consequences and have various causes. For example, the composition of the atmosphere affects the formation of an ice age. Between 1600 and 1800, there was a 'little ice age' in Europe. At this time, temperatures were one to two degrees lower than they are today.

ICE CAP — Permanent layer of snow and ice. The two largest ice caps in the world are the Greenland and Antarctic ice caps.

INCAS — Native population that lived in the western part of South America in the Andes until roughly the middle of the sixteenth century.

INDUSTRIAL REVOLUTION — The Industrial Revolution began at the end of the eighteenth century in England and followed in the rest of Europe during the nineteenth century. This period saw the conversion from the manual to mechanised production of goods. The steam engine played an important role. The first factories were created and industrialisation also led to the establishment of the first cities.

INDUSTRIALISATION — The process of technological changes in production processes, through extensive mechanisation and the social implications of this, which occurred during the period of the Industrial Revolution.

INFRARED RADIATION — Electromagnetic radiation which is not visible to the naked eye, though we do feel it thanks to its warming effect.

INTELLECTUAL PROPERTY — Collective name for a number of rights to products of the human spirit. Examples include copyright, patent, trademark and trade name rights.

IPCC — Intergovernmental Panel on Climate Change, an international organisation that studies climate change.

JAGA EXPERIENCE LAB — Scientific testing centre and open workshop at Jaga in Diepenbeek where technical, economic and creative minds can come together to think of innovative solutions to climate change.

KIRIBATI — Kiribati is a country in Oceania which consists of several groups of islands in the Pacific Ocean. Large parts of Kiribati are threatened by the effects of global warming.

KNOWLEDGE ECONOMY (THE) — The part of the economy that is associated with knowledge instead of the traditional production factors of work, nature, and capital.

LIFE CYCLE ASSESSMENT (LCA) — Method for determining the total impact of a product on the environment during its entire life cycle: from the extraction of raw materials to production, transport, consumption and waste processing.

LIVING PLANET INDEX Indicator of biodiversity on earth. The index has been measured since 1997 and was commissioned by the World Wildlife Fund. It provides an insight into our living environment and the evolution of biodiversity.

MASLOW, ABRAHAM American psychologist who introduced the concept of the hierarchy of needs in *A Theory of Human Motivation* (1943).

MESSAGE OUT OF THE FUTURE Name of the book and the film made by the Uchronia Community about its participation in the Burning Man event of 2006.

METHANE Methane (CH_4) is the simplest hydrocarbon and belongs to the alkanes group. It is the main component of natural gas and is found in its natural form with fossil fuels such as petroleum. It is also emitted by livestock. Methane is considered to be one of the greenhouse gases.

MOBY The modular oxygen bubble is a visionary concept by Jaga: a self-sustaining bubble with the perfect oxygen and CO_2 levels and reduced energy consumption. The prototype is a high-tech interactive multimedia vehicle in which users can sleep, read, work, travel, socialise ...

NEW GLOBAL ECONOMIES Collective name for the countries whose economies have grown significantly in recent years, such as China, Brazil and India. These new world economies are seen as competition for the Western economy.

PATENT A patent is an exclusive right that a government grants to a person or company to make or sell a particular article or to exploit a specific invention.

OECD Organisation for Economic Cooperation and Development.

OLYMPUS At 2,917 metres, the Olympus is the highest mountain in Greece. It is located in the southwest of Thessaloniki and plays an important role in Greek mythology. Olympus was the home of the supreme god Zeus.

OPEN GREENFORCE

Independent consultancy and centre for expertise for sustainable innovation. Shares knowledge with Greenforce on the development of technology and products.

OPEN INNOVATION

An economic system in which knowledge is not protected within a company, a country or an organisation, but is shared in order to make collective progress possible.

OZONE LAYER

Layer in the atmosphere – at an altitude of between 15 and 45 km – which contains a lot of ozone. That ozone is caused by oxygen molecules splitting under the influence of ultraviolet radiation.

PANDORA

In Greek mythology, Pandora was the name of the first woman. Hephaestus created her from water and earth; the gods gave her many gifts. She was given to the people by Zeus to bring doom and disaster upon the earth. That disaster was hidden in a box that Pandora opened out of curiosity.

PERMAFROST

The ground beneath the surface layer that is always frozen and can be found in approximately one fifth of the earth's surface, especially near the poles and in the mountains.

PHOTOSYNTHESIS

The process by which light energy turns carbon dioxide into carbohydrates. Photosynthesis in plants and oceans produces oxygen.

PLANTAGON GREENHOUSE

'Vegetal skyscraper'. A unique feeding system designed by Swedish scientists and visionary thinkers with the intention of reducing the constant supply of raw materials, energy and water to cities.

PLASTIC ARCHIPELAGO

Term for the large amount of pieces of plastic floating around together in the North Pacific Ocean and impacting biodiversity in the area.

POLAR CONSERVATION ORGANISATION

Non-profit organisation that aims to create a sustainable future for the Polar Regions.

PRECAMBRIAN

Time period before the Cambrian, used to describe the geological history of the earth. The Precambrian begins with the earth's creation (4,560 million years ago) and lasted about 4 billion years.

PRODUCT EXPERIENCE DAYS	Special 'experience branding' days held at Jaga during which both internal and external employees can present their ideas for climate change solutions and radiator concepts.
PROMETHEUS	Prometheus is an important figure from Greek mythology and the son of a titan. After he had stolen fire from the gods and given it to humans, Zeus punished him and all of humanity.
PROSUMPTION	Term from Alvin Toffler. Aggregation of *proactive* and *consumption* which refers to the consumer playing an active role in the development of products or services, thus becoming more than just a consumer.
SCHUITEN, LUC	Brussels' visionary architect who designs 'vegetal cities'.
STEGER, WILL	Founder of the Will Steger Foundation. He has completed legendary polar expeditions and in so doing became an eyewitness to the effects of climate change.
TECTONIC PLATE	A piece of the earth's crust. The earth's surface consists of six major tectonic plates and several smaller ones. They move at a slow pace.
TOFFLER, ALVIN	American futurologist who studies changes in contemporary society and predicts future trends based on his findings. He wrote *Third Wave*, a book that predicts the end of mass consumption and the beginning of personalised products.
UCHRONIA	Work of art created by the Uchronia Community in 2006 at Burning Man.
UCHRONIA COMMUNITY	Creative platform, founded in 2006, which aims to combine all archetypes to create a universal survival model based on the principle of the creative economy.
UCHRONIAN	Member of the Uchronia Community.
UCHRONIAN ARC	The arc that Uchronians used in 2009 to travel to the Copenhagen Climate Change Conference and to which they invited eyewitnesses of global warming.
UV RADIATION	Ultraviolet radiation is electromagnetic radiation that is not visible to the naked eye. Along with visible light, the

sun also emits ultraviolet rays that can burn the skin. The particles and ozone in the atmosphere affect the amount of ultraviolet sunlight that reaches the earth.

UNITED NATIONS

International organisation founded in 1945, which works in many fields, including justice, security and human rights and which also holds climate change conferences.

VAN MECHELEN, KOEN

Belgian conceptual artist who became famous for the Cosmopolitan Chicken Project. He collaborates with scientists from all over the world.

VREDESEILANDEN

An independent Belgian development organisation that supports programmes in Africa, Asia, Latin America and Flanders.

WATER FOOTPRINT

The amount of water needed to make a product, from the mining of raw materials to the final product for the consumer.

WEARABLE HEATING

Collective name for several Jaga heating concepts that don't heat up and cool down people's surroundings, but rather people themselves.

WORLD WILDLIFE FUND

International non-profit organisation which aims to create a world in which humans live in harmony with nature.

ZERO CARBON EMISSION

The objective of clean technology: no more carbon dioxide emissions.

ZEUS

Important figure from Greek mythology. He was the supreme god and lived on Mount Olympus.

INTERESTING BOOKS AND WEBSITES

Books

Al Gore, *Onze keuze - Een actieplan om het klimaat te redden*, Meulenhoff, 2009.
Alvin Toffler, *The Third Wave*, Pan Books, 1980.
Michael Braungart and William McDonough, *Cradle to Cradle – Afval = voedsel*, Search Knowledge, 2007.
Pier Vellinga, *Hoezo Klimaatverandering*, Balans, 2011.
Richard Florida, *The Rise of the Creative Class*, Basic Books, 2002.
Uchonia Community, Message from the future, 2006.

Websites

Al Gore: www.algore.com
De Morgen – Planet Watch: http://www.demorgen.be/dm/nl/5376/Planet-Watch/index.dhtml
Dirk Claesen: www.zephyr-wildlife.be
Environmental Protection Encouragement Agency: www.epea.com
Grupo Torcello: www.grupotorcello.com
Intergovernmental Panel on Climate Change: www.ipcc.ch
Koen Van Mechelen: www.koenvanmechelen.be
National Geographic: www.nationalgeographic.com
Open Greenforce: www.opengreenforce.com
Greenforce Belgium: www.greenforcebelgium.com
Polar Conservation Organisation: www.polarconservation.org
Richard Florida: www.creativeclass.com
Uchronia Community: www.uchronians.org
Vincent Callebaut: www.vincent.callebaut.org
Watervoetafdruk: www.watervoetafdruk.be en www.waterfootprint.org
Wereld Natuur Fonds – Ecologische voetafdruk berekenen: www.wwf-footprint.be
Wereld Natuur Fonds: www.wwf.be
Will Steger Foundation: www.willsteger.com
Geronimo, Jumping Bull: www.thejumpingbull.com
Jaga: www.theradiatorfactory.com
Jaga Experience Lab: www.jagaexperiencelab.com
Jan Kriekels: www.jankriekels.be

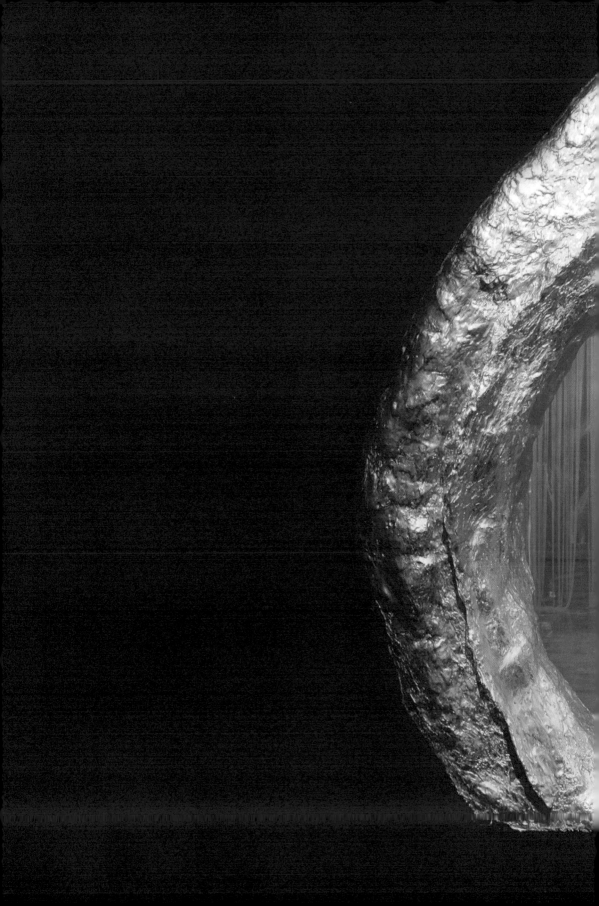

TRANSFORMATION GATEWAY FOR ENTREPRENEURS